WRITING
FROM WITHIN

"Very deep . . .
very deep is the well
of the past."

Thomas Mann
Joseph and His Brothers

Other books and films by Bernard Selling:

Writing From Within: A Teaching Guide
Best Autobiographical Stories from Life Story Writing Classes
The Flying Machine (from a story by Ray Bradbury)
Three Miraculous Soldiers (from a story by Stephen Crane)
First Year A.D.
Little Train
Henry

◊ ◊ ◊

To Lowell and Mary,
my parents

Writing From Within

A Unique Guide
to Writing Your Life's Stories

◊ ◊ ◊ ◊ ◊

BERNARD SELLING

First U.S. classroom edition published in 1988, first U.S. paperback edition published in 1989, second (revised) U.S. edition published in 1990 by Hunter House Inc., Publishers.

Hunter House Inc., Publishers
P.O. Box 847
Claremont CA 91711

Library of Congress Cataloging-in-Publication Data

Selling, Bernard
　　Writing from within: a unique guide to writing your life's stories / Bernard Selling. — 2nd ed.
　　　p. cm.
　　Includes bibliographical references: p.268
　　ISBN 0-89793-079-7 : $11.95
　　1. Autobiography.　2. United States—Biography.　I. Title

0CT25.S45　1990
808'.06692—dc20　　　　　　　　　　　　　　　　　　　-90-47964
　　　　　　　　　　　　　　　　　　　　　　　　　　　　CIP

Book design by Furbeyre & Associates
Cover design by Teri Robertson
Copy editing by Jackie Melvin & Kiran Rana
Editorial coordinator: Corrine Sahli
Production by Paul Frindt
Set in 11 on 13 point Century Schoolbook by 847 Communications,
　　Claremont, CA
Printed by Delta Lithograph Co., Valencia, CA
Manufactured in the United States of America
9 8 7 6 5 4 3 2 1　　　　　　Second edition

TABLE OF CONTENTS

PREFACE

WHEN I WAS SIXTEEN YEARS OLD, MY FATHER DIED—
an expected and painful event for me. He was an
enigma: a prominent psychiatrist, the possessor of
seven college degrees, an angry and charming man,
highly ethical, overbearing, and accomplished. A heart
attack eight years before his death caused him to stumble
toward the finish line of his life like an exhausted mar-
athon runner whose sole purpose in life was to stay
alive until his children finished high school. He almost
made it.

For weeks after his death, I read copies of all the
letters he wrote during his years of public life. Nowhere
could I find anything personal about him: who he was,
where he had come from, where he thought he was going.

Beyond a few facts and remembrances and a few
funny stories, I knew very little. My mother died a few
years after my father and I reached young adulthood in
the 1950s feeling like an existential antihero—free to
make choices but not guided by an immediate past or a
family history—truly alone.

In the intervening years, from Dad's death until
the present, my father's sister, the one person who could
reveal more of him, showed no interest in telling me more
of his life, particularly his thoughts and feelings.

"People of our generation do not dwell on such
things," she would say. "I don't have time." So it appeared

that my father's history, both family and personal, would remain shrouded in darkness, consigned to oblivion. And indeed it has come to pass. This has saddened me enormously.

When asked to teach the classes from which this book was drawn, I thought how much it would have meant to me to know my parents well: how they were raised, the things they did, and, most of all, what they thought and felt as they experienced their lives. This became my touchstone for teaching the class—actions and events accurately described, feelings about them honestly and vividly captured.

As the classes developed over several years, I began to realize the importance of what we were accomplishing.

First of all, the writing process was immensely therapeutic for each person. It was plain to see that once the participants had overcome a fear of writing, the process of getting their life stories out and on paper had a revitalizing effect on them.

Second, being congratulated for good work and encouraged by class members to keep at the task was equally therapeutic and informative.

Third, the warm acceptance of their work by family members revealed to each person that he or she was filling a genuine need within the family.

Fourth, and most inspiring, was the awareness that, as each writer became more skilled, the quality of his or her legacy would itself become a touchstone for the family and inspire histories to be written by generations yet unborn. Occasionally, someone would comment after a particularly good story, "What would it be like for us if our parents and forebears had left memories as well-written and revealing as the stories coming to the surface in our workshop?"

Ultimately, this is the great lure of life story writing: to be able to affect the future of the families into which we are born; to give direction, amusement, and perspective to our children's children and their children; to write so well that a hundred years from now those who follow can clearly see the footprints that we made and can begin to gauge their own paths by our direction.

I would like to thank Betty Springer and Gyl Roland for their support, advice, and encouragement, and Ruth Tachna for her editorial assistance with this volume. I would of course like to thank the students in my life story writing classes, without whom this volume could not have been written. To Jack Garfein, who heads the Actors and Directors Lab in Los Angeles and New York, I must also express my gratitude, for it was in his acting, directing, and writing classes that I learned the Stanislavski approach to drama, an approach that has inspired many of the techniques I use in my writing classes.

Following the publication of the first edition of this book, I received a great deal of valuable feedback about its effectiveness. A number of people responded strongly to the personal glimpses I had given my readers, so in this edition I have tried to provide a few more where they make my teaching a little clearer.

Some new techniques I developed that have become central to my teaching, such as "Finding the Beginning" and "Expanding the Climax," are included here. I also found that the feedback and rewriting processes, as well as the process of writing from a child's point of view, which is the very core of the life story writing approach, needed expansion and development. The reader will find out more about each of these processes in this second edition.

As I presented my workshops around the country, I found people were greatly interested in the unexpected and often unusual benefits of life story writing. The reader will, therefore, find at the end of Part II a discussion of these benefits, including those to individual writers, to the curricula of our school system, and to the counseling and healing professions.

Finally, about half of the stories from the first edition have been replaced by ones with greater impact, or which more accurately reflect my approach to life story writing.

I would like to give special thanks to my editor at Hunter House, Jackie Melvin, for all her work on this edition. Her sharp eye and sensitivity to the material improved the book tremendously.

Bernard Selling
Venice, California, 1990

INTRODUCTION

FOR MANY YEARS, OBSERVERS OF AMERICAN CULTURE— David Riesman, Alvin Toffler, and others—have noted the rootlessness and materialism of our society as well as its loosening connections to its own past, and they have examined with care the catalysts of this rootlessness, the upwardly mobile American middle class. None of these observers, however, has paid much attention to the patterns of life of those left behind: parents and grandparents.

But over the past ten years, we have seen a distinct shift toward respect for roots. And with it, an increasing respect for the wit and wisdom of those who have gotten us where we are—those same parents and grandparents. For a writer and teacher who works with mature adults, this is a welcome change.

This volume is written for those who wish to inform their children and grandchildren about the life path that they, the writers, have followed. It is a self-help text, derived from the life story writing classes and workshops I have been teaching.

The book is in three parts. Part I exposes the writer to various techniques that will help him learn to express himself fully and well on paper (—or "her... herself"—until our language finds a good word that includes both sexes, we writers have to make certain choices. The use of he, him, etc. in the text is a convention only and emphatically includes the female).

Part II guides the writer toward certain questions and life experiences his children and grandchildren will want to know about. One chapter is devoted to questions that can be asked of those interested in having their oral history recorded.

Some of you may wish to read this oral history section first; the questions may provoke you to recollect stories and incidents from your past.

The closing chapter in Part II discusses the many and unusual benefits to be gained from carrying out the task of writing one's life stories.

Part III is composed of selections from our life story writing classes that demonstrate the various techniques we have developed and discussed. These techniques allow the reader a much more intimate sense of the writer's thoughts, feelings, and experiences than is normally the case in journal writing, oral history, and life narrative writing. The selections give a real taste of what we mean by "writing from within"— finding and capturing on paper the way life unfolded in vivid, emotional, intimate detail, experienced from the point of view of the writer at the age when the events occurred.

Some may wish to read this book through from beginning to end before starting to write. In that case, you may wish to jot down notes as ideas, incidents, and people from the past come to mind.

I encourage you to go at the work in a leisurely manner. There is no need to rush through. It may take weeks or even months to move from one chapter to the next. That is to be expected. How many stories you do in each chapter is very much up to you. You may well take six months to a year, or longer, to work through the book.

In the first few weeks and months, you will be spending a great deal of time rewriting, time that you might prefer to spend on the next recollection. To get the intimacy and depth of feeling and observation which is possible using the techniques described in the book, allow yourself the extra time and effort. Reread the book several times. In doing this, you will gradually make the techniques you have read and thought about a part of you. Using them will begin to feel comfortable. You will be happy with the results.

You will notice also that at the end of each section on composing I include a short personal note to you. It is intended to guide you into the actual writing, for I do urge you to begin writing when I say *now*. Don't bother fussing, worrying, or protesting. Whatever comes out is a first draft, which can be revised later. If you wish to read through the whole book before beginning to write, that is fine. Go ahead. But do allow the book to help you get down to the task of writing, not thinking about writing.

I am often asked, "Should I write my stories chronologically or should I write as my inner urge dictates?" By all means, write as that inner urge dictates. Your stories ought, generally, to be arranged in chronological order if you print or publish them, but you, as the writer, need feel no compulsion to *write* them in that order. The vivid memories are the ones most likely to pop out at you at any time of the day or night.

I do suggest that you write several early memories first, learning to write from the child's point of view before skipping around and writing about different phases of your life. Writing a number of early memories enables you to start with simpler memories and to discover the power of writing "authentically," that is, writing in a voice that is consistent with the age of the person you were. By getting back to that person, you will discover much of your past that you have forgotten or remembered inaccurately.

The style you will be developing will be forceful, immediate, and intimate. It will be full of dialogue and your inner thoughts and feelings. You will be developing your own authentic writer's voice, while you learn how to "write from within."

PART ONE

ACQUIRING THE TECHNIQUES

CHAPTER ONE

OVERCOMING FEAR

To TELL ONE'S LIFE STORIES, TO LEAVE A MEMOIR OF the sad/happy, exciting/boring, fascinating/fearful experiences of one's long life seems like a wonderful idea. But how many wonderful ideas have we had in our lives which never became anything more than ideas? Quite a few? Yes, I suppose so. What stopped them from becoming reality? Probably lack of motivation or fear... or both.

If the idea of writing your own life story strikes a chord within you, sets off a bell, causes you to salivate —or fills you with unspeakable dread—then you are ready to write your story. What is holding you back is not lack of motivation. It is fear. Stark, naked fear.

Fear of what? Fear of being unable to write well and being criticized by friends and relatives? Fear of being unable to finish, of getting off the track? Fear that we might say too much and embarrass someone? Fear that we may dig up old painful "stuff" that we can't handle? Fear that we just don't have what it takes to write well?

Research into the way the brain operates suggests

that there are two sides to the brain—left and right. Much of our fear of writing comes from the way these two sides do or don't work together.

We might term the right brain "the creator," for apparently it allows us to do creative things—make connections, create ideas, imagine situations of all kinds, see pictures of events. The left side analyzes things, puts them into categories, recalls words, and performs its learning functions in a step-by-step manner.

For our purposes, what is important to know is that the analytic left brain has a little attic up on top which houses the "critic." He—or she—is the person in us who says, "Watch out! You can't do that! You'll fail, so don't even try. You know you're no good at that!"

And perhaps you would be right if you said that the critic sounds a lot like dear old Mom or Dad: "If I've told you once, I've told you a thousand times, you may not do (something you really *want* to do) until you have carried out the garbage"—or cleaned out your room, done the dishes, gotten good grades, etc. Sound familiar? I'm sure it does. Believe me, I know. I, too, am a parent . . . and remember being a child.

Well, parents are great, but they do tend to be critical. They are our guides in the world, but too often they do more than guide us. They tell us not to do certain things and we become afraid to do them.

The critic becomes a problem for us when we want to create something out of nothing—let's say a story or a painting—because the right brain, in which our "creator" stirs every now and then, is very tender, very sensitive to criticism. So if our left-side, tough-minded, parent-critic brain says, "Forget it! You can't do it," our right-side, tender-minded creator says, "Fine! OK! I'm going back to sleep. Talk to me again in a few weeks."

And so our deep desire to create—in this case, to write our life's stories—gets buried once again.

How do we counteract the critic? We calm him. We

stroke him. When he comes out, we become aware of his presence but we do not fight him. We can enjoy his antics, be amused by his swordplay as he cuts away at our confidence, but we must keep out of range of that slashing saber. And we must avoid a confrontational stance with the critic: "What do you mean I can't do it! I can so!!" To the critic, that is merely a call to arms. On the other hand, a flexible stance—something like "You'll be surprised what I can do," or "I've been doing pretty well, so I think I'll keep on creating, even if it seems kind of hard"—will deflect the critic's thrusts and keep our creative juices flowing. So enjoy the critic, be amused by him, but don't try to duel with him. He is actually valuable at a later stage when he is calmer and able to look at your work objectively. He can then suggest ways and means of changing and editing it.

We human beings have an almost infinite variety of ways to censor ourselves. Fear not only keeps us from writing, it inhibits us from letting the world see our work when it is done. We tend to be very hard on ourselves as writers. In fact, some very good work may be lost because of our pessimism.

The following is an example of a fine story that the writer had tossed in the garbage. The writer revealed what he had done, and the class responded by insisting that he resurrect the story and bring it in. Here it is, complete with stains from coffee grounds and fried eggs.

MY FRIEND JAKE
by David Yavitts

From a small town in eastern Russia, our family arrived in the midwest of the United States, in St. Paul, Minnesota, a short distance from the banks of the Mississippi River.

Our house was on two and a half acres, partly in a hollow. The front of the house, that is, the parlor, living room and dining room, were on street level. The kitchen and bedroom were on the hollow portion, held up by posts.

It was there that life for me began in this country. In the next couple of years, we had acquired a cow, horse, chickens and ducks. My responsibility was the ducks, keeping their quarters clean and feeding them.

I became very fond of them, gave them names and learned to recognize them by color and size. My favorite duck I called Jake, because we got that particular duck from our neighbor Jake's farm.

As I spoke the English language poorly, I did not have any friends, and I adopted Jake as my friend and confidant. He listened to me and would cock his head and did not move until I was through speaking. He would always wait for a while.

Jake grew faster than the other ducks and his feathers, especially around his neck, were a ring of black. The rest was white.

That winter the ducks became full grown and plump. In the spring, I was assisting my mother in cleaning the stove pipes. They were full of soot and as I removed the soot much of the black powder made my face and hands black.

It was time to feed the ducks and I couldn't find Jake, my duck. I looked everywhere and called him. There wasn't any response. I finally went into the house; my mother was at the stove baking what she said was a chicken. I explained to her that Jake, my duck, was lost and that I couldn't find him. My mother told me, if the duck was lost she would get me another one—not to worry!

At this point, my older sister came in the kitchen and said, "Is the duck done yet?"

The sky fell down and I shouted, "That's Jake!" They could not pacify me. I cried and told them they were mean and bad to kill Jake and I ran out of the house, saying I didn't want to live there any more. I said I was going to my uncle's house across the bridge, over the river.

They didn't believe it, but I started my journey.

I knew where the bridge was; I could see it from my home and headed in that direction. Here was a dirty-faced kid about three and a half who cried as he walked toward the bridge. In my mind, I knew my soft-hearted uncle would solve my problems.

Well, I didn't get very far on the bridge when I was stopped by a policeman who asked, "Where are you going, young man?"

He repeated that question many times. I did not understand too well. I spoke Yiddish and that soft-hearted Irish policeman spoke English with a brogue. He took me to the police station. There, an officer who understood me got my story, figured out where I lived, left me at the station and eventually called my mother. She got my older sister out of the class-room at school and sent her to the station. My sister thought she would have to bail me out. There I was, my sister said, sitting on a table with an ice cream cone in my hand and crying. The tears ran down my face, washing the black soot off in white streaks. The ice cream washed my lips. I was a sight! My mother said, "Come home, dinner is waiting."

I said, "Mother, I don't eat duck!"

◊ ◊ ◊

Having read the story, we can see it is complete and effective. The detail and observations are sharp; the dialogue is appropriate. It has a beginning, a mid-dle, and an end; it is personal and deeply felt. Yet, despite its obvious excellence, the writer had dumped it in the trash. Imagine what would have happened, not only to the story, but also to the man's future as a writer, had the class not insisted that he retrieve it.

Once we understand how our left-brain critic works, we can begin to work on our memoirs knowing we can defuse our fears by identifying the pressure of the critic when he appears.

You may say, "I don't really have any fear and I don't think I have much of a critic." That's wonderful. But let's give ourselves a little test in order to find out. Let's suppose we've been given a writing task and have about a paragraph written. Myself, I am inclined to stop at this point and go over what I've written. What about you? Do you go on? Or do you keep working on this paragraph until you feel it is correct? In the next chapter we will see what the answer to this question tells us about ourselves and our critic. We will also begin to work on our first life story.

Chapter Two

Finding Your
Earliest Memories

Let's begin writing" —these are words calcu-lated to strike fear into the heartiest of souls, par-ticularly those who may not have touched pen to paper in many years. Calm yourself. The writing process need not be traumatic. In fact, it can be fun. *Thinking* about writing (or, really, *worrying* about it) can be traumatic. So let's not think about it right now. Let's do it.

"All right," you say, "suppose I have calmed my fears. What do I write about? My life is dull, dull, dull." The answer is that no life is dull; only the way it is remembered and recorded is dull. We must find the ways and means of getting to the interesting events and people in our lives in a manner that is comfortable for us, and real.

There are essentially three phases to writing a memoir in an interesting, authentic way: composing it, reviewing it, and rewriting it. By following the specific steps that are part of each phase, you can be assured that your work will be readable and enjoyable.

Some of you may want to start by writing the life

stories of your parents and grandparents. "They came first, so shouldn't I write what I know about them first?" you ask. The answer is: probably not. It is important to keep the family past distinct from your personal life story. Also, the quality of your writing about others will improve if you wait until you have developed your life story writing skills.

So, the answer to your question, "What do I write about?" is, "Write your earliest memory first." Your earliest memory is a good place to begin because it is something you see in your mind's eye, but it is not too complex to describe. It will probably be a fragment of something, a piece of a picture. That is just fine. It does not have to be a story. Even a few lines will do. It's like doing "Twinkle, Twinkle, Little Star" when you were first learning to play the piano.

You may be surprised how interesting, revealing, and important that little fragment really is. One of my students had been told all her life that she had hit her baby sister over the head with her bottle. What a traumatic memory to live with! But when she went way back to the actual incident, she recalled hitting the bottle on the side of the crib, and the bottle breaking and then hitting her sister. Suddenly, she was relieved of a guilt that had haunted her all her life, and the relief was wonderful!

Earliest memories are often dramatic—a birth or death in the family, leaving or arriving at someplace special, a medical emergency. Sometimes, though, they can be as simple as remembering a shiny thing that hung over your crib. No matter how simple, write down what you see in your mind. Just that. Nothing more.

COMPOSING

Composing is the first phase of writing your life stories, and it involves the following:

Choose a comfortable place and time

Find a quiet, comfortable place in which you can work undisturbed (although European writers often prefer outdoor cafés where the noise seems to be strangely comforting); something relaxing in which to sit—a bed or a chair; a place where the light is adequate and not distracting. It is equally important to find the right time to write—usually sometime between eight in the evening and noon the next day. Our right-brain creativity is most at work during these times, whereas during the afternoon our left-brain, analytical energies are highest. So, if you don't feel like writing in the afternoon, don't force it.

Select a few familiar objects

Surround yourself with familiar objects which will remind you of your earliest experiences in life—photos, clothing, and other mementos of your past.

Relax

Let us assume that having accomplished the first two steps, you are now trying to think. Perhaps you find yourself getting a little sleepy. You resist the urge, battling it for ten or fifteen minutes until finally you fall asleep. You awaken some time later feeling depressed; you have let yourself down. But you really have not. The next time this urge to sleep strikes you, give in to it. It's OK. It is your brain's way of switching from the everyday, problem-solving, left-brain mode to the creative, right-brain mode.

Return to the past

Use your daydream or reverie to channel your thoughts back toward the deep past. Now that you are comfortable and relaxed, and perhaps semi-sleepy, allow your mind to float back in time, way back to your first memory. It really doesn't matter whether you were three months old or three years old. It doesn't matter if it is not a story. It may be just a fragment of a picture. That is fine, as long as you *see* something.

Start writing and keep on writing

Once you have begun your story, keep writing. Resist the urge to go back and make that first paragraph perfect. That urge is your "critic" speaking. Just plunge on. Don't stop.

Write from a child's point of view

Write down what you have just seen in your mind's eye from the point of view of the baby or child you once were. If you were in a crib, the reader would expect to see a bit of the crib sticking up at the foot of the bed where Momma and Poppa might be staring down at you. Create a strong and vivid picture of what you see: the place where the event is occurring, the sounds and smells around you, and the atmosphere of the scene. It is important to record all of these details. Seeing the world through the eyes of a child, when the world was new and fresh, makes fascinating reading.

Here are some topics that may trigger your earliest memories:

— My earliest happy experience

— My earliest sad or shocking experience

— My first experience with a birth in the family

— My first experience with a death in the family

— My first day in school or the first day I remember in school

— My first experience of being all alone without Mommy or Daddy

— My first experience in the hospital—tonsils out, other illness

— My first experience eating, or playing, or riding on a train, bus, etc.

◊ ◊ ◊

I know what to do, so it is time to do it. I am ready to begin. I am in a favorite, comfortable place. There are no distractions. It is quiet outside and in. There are important objects around me and I may even be a bit sleepy. My mind begins to drift back, way back. I am very relaxed. I am beginning to see the first thing that I remember.... I am going to write it **now**.

REVIEWING

Having found your earliest memory and having written a first draft of it, you have completed the initial writing phase. The next phase is to review what you have done to see how your work comes across to a listener or reader. Like composing, the reviewing phase has several steps.

Resist the urge to make changes

The urge to make big changes and to be critical is always strong at this point. ("It *can't* be any good—I better change it.") Resist that temptation. Read over the story and make only a few corrections, such as cleaning up grammar and spelling. What you need most at this point is some feedback about the quality and effectiveness of what you have written.

Get feedback

Now you need to get some responses from friends about what you have written. It's rather scary to ask for reactions, but it will turn out OK. My own preference is to have a friend review it. A relative may be either too critical or too patronizing, and neither of these attitudes is helpful for a beginning writer. So find a friend and read it aloud to him or her. (See Chapter Seven, "Developing Supportive Feedback," for assistance on how to do this.)

Form a group

Working with a group of friends or acquaintances who are also interested in writing their life stories is very desirable, for several reasons. Reading memoirs aloud to a group will tell you whether your stories are coming across well or not. It is also fun to share remembrances of the past with friends, and often someone else's stories will remind you about similar experiences of your own. Another reason is that sharing stories with friends who are also interested in writing is less intimidating—everyone knows that his or her writing will be reviewed.

Write visually, for impact

Ask those who listen to your stories two things: Are the stories visual (can they see them clearly in their minds)? and, Do they have an emotional impact (what do the listeners feel as they listen to them)? Usually, if the story has an impact, the listeners will tell you it reminded them of a similar time in their own lives. This is a very good sign.

Listen to yourself

Very often, you, the writer, will respond to comments, both positive and negative, by mentioning incidents, colors, objects, observations and reflections which you consciously or unconsciously decided to leave out. This is almost always vital information which needs to be in the story. So listen to yourself in class or with your friends, and flesh out the story with this information.

Achieve a "childlike" tone

Become aware of your story as a moment in time seen and experienced by a child. The story needs to have simple vocabulary, reasonably short sentences, and, above all, it needs to be visual. Everything in it needs to be clear.

You now know the six steps to follow to review and evaluate your memoir. Here is an example of an earliest memory.

CATERPILLAR

by Gina Wilcox

It was springtime, so I was about a year and three months old. We sat on the cement steps in front of our flat at 5959 Justine Street, Chicago. Mama plopped me down on the sidewalk and turned to gossip with shiny Aunt Rose. I could walk fast and slow, and do falling down and getting up all by myself. The smell of tar was very strong. The leaves of the tree had a lesser smell. They were oval shaped, coming to a point at the bottom with little stickers all around the edge. They seemed to have a life of their own. Each leaf came down in some other way of falling to me. Then that crawling thing began playing with me. A concertina shaped creature with fuzzy black hair and some yellow down around lots of little pointy feet. This piece of real live something bumped itself up to the middle, looked around, and proceeded. Bump up, look around, proceed; bump up, look around, proceed. Slowly and deliberately. It was like grandpa who sometimes had to walk with a slow hunch. When he did ᵗʰᵃᵗ right, you could hear by his grunts that it ᵂᵃˢⁿ't hurting him. That was like this small moving creature. I didn't know what "caterpillar" was, so I did the only sensible thing I knew. I picked it up and put it in my mouth, or tried to. It wiggled out of my clutches. I followed, watching more carefully. When I felt the timing was right, I grabbed with my entire fist and squeezed. Some of the hairs came through between my fingers. It tickled. I dropped it. Off again! Gone into the cinders around the strong smelling tree. Mama called: *"Sto je ovo? Hodi ti simo!"* (What's going on? Come this minute!) I explained to her that I had discovered delicious moving things to play with and how happy I was.

◊ ◊ ◊

Notice how Gina allows us to experience all the sights, smells, tastes, and textures of things that are new and wonderful to a child, sensations that we as adults just take for granted. But Gina's story doesn't really sound as if a child were doing the experiencing, does it? There is a great deal of vocabulary that is clearly adult and keeps us out of the story somewhat, even though the sense of innocence and wonder is strong.

REWRITING

We are now at the final phase of putting together your first memoir: rewriting. The first phase, composing, involved freeing you up to get your story down on paper without stopping, that is, without letting the critic grab hold of you and drag you back to redo that first paragraph, as so often happens. The second phase, reviewing, involved helping you to get some objective feedback about your work by having a friend or group listen and respond to it. In the final phase, rewriting, you will learn how to make your story more vivid and substantially clearer to the reader, while deepening its impact.

Later on we will explore rewriting more thoroughly, but this first memoir needs only a bit of tinkering to make it work. It is, after all, just a moment from your childhood, probably not even a complete story. Like a pianist learning to play the scales, a note at a time, your present task is only to make this moment dramatic and believable.

When rewriting this first memoir, then, keep these guidelines in mind.

Write visually

Be sure the story is made visible, with clear, vivid details.

Create emotional impact

Be aware of what your feelings were. Do you remember them? If you do, add in reactions like, "I felt scared," "I felt happy," etc.

Write from a child's point of view

This is perhaps the most important consideration for this early story: Be sure your memoir sounds as if it were experienced by a child.

You are probably asking, "How in the world can I write as a child would when I'm not a child? Shouldn't I just write as an adult looking back?"

The answer is: "No." You may not be able to write exactly as a child would, but you can avoid certain writing patterns which mark the passages as those of an adult. You are, after all, trying to recapture the world as seen through a child's eyes, not an adult's eyes. Avoid using vocabulary, diction, and phrasing that a child could not possibly use. For example, consider the following passage:

> There were times, I suppose, when it seemed as if one would never be permitted to mature at a

pace which was reasonable for my age. No, I was forced, albeit in a kindly fashion, to repeat ad nauseam the chores and duties attendant upon childhood: taking out the garbage, playing sports, minding my manners and obeying the strictures of my parents.

No one reading this passage would suppose for a moment that a child had written it. Why? Because children don't talk or write that way. Let us look at specific parts of this passage to see what is unchildlike about it.

Vocabulary and phrasing: "permitted to mature," "reasonable for my age," "ad nauseam," "attendant upon" are all phrases no child, other than one attending college at a remarkably early age, would ever use.

Qualifications: Statements that are qualified or modified are virtually never used by children. "I suppose" is a qualification, as is "albeit in a nice way."

The objective voice: "One" is the objective voice and is virtually never used by children.

Lists: Cataloging chores, etc., in an orderly manner is an adult way of organizing. Children may do it, but they are less orderly and logical.

Now, let us look at the passage after rewriting it in a way that may not be childlike but at least is not obviously adult.

From the time I was six or seven until I was eleven, my dad insisted that I take out the garbage every Thursday. What a chore that was! It seemed as if he'd never give me any real responsibility, just chores. But I remember one time when he . . .

Here you have a voice that could be adult or child. The passage is simple, straightforward, and visual. The narrator's voice and point of view do not intrude on the action or the progress of the story.

So that the reader can see the differences between a childhood story and a rewrite told exclusively from a child's point of view, the first and second drafts of a story by Jade are given below.

WILLEM (1)

by Jade

I have no recollection of the first years of my life. Looking way back into my early childhood, I come up with this little picture, a picture that has surfaced every once in a while whenever I am thinking of the old days.

I must have been three or four. There was a big sprawling backyard. A tall hedge concealed the main house, some distance away. The house was quiet; my mother must be resting. It was siesta time, the time after lunch when the shimmering tropical heat made people drowsy. It was also Sunday, the drone of my father's machines was not there. My father must also be resting. My father had a house-industry at that time. He bought up spices such as pepper, nutmeg, cloves, cinnamon, etc. from the farmers overseas on the other island, then he ground and bottled them in a special building on the grounds. To assist him he asked Willem to come over from his hometown on a far island to work as his foreman. Willem also lived with us in an outhouse.

I liked Willem, because he always spent time with us, whenever there was a chance. That afternoon was no exception. He showed my brother and me some magic tricks and then he said, "Kids, I am going to show you how strong I am!" He asked Joni, another workman, to go fetch the bicycle. Then he lay down on the grass and Joni was told to drive over his chest. I was greatly impressed when Willem stood up unhurt. Then he said, "And now the van will drive over me." Again he lay down on the thick grass and supposedly the car drove over him. I was in awe that nothing happened to Willem. This was where I got befuddled. I am sure I had not told my mother then and there, because she would have taken some action regarding Willem's way of entertaining us and she would have remembered the incident. As it was, when years later I talked about it, mother said, "Nonsense, he must have tricked you." But I still wonder, did it really happen or was it just my imagination?

◊ ◊ ◊

After hearing the story, members of the class suggested that she simplify the vocabulary and tell the story exclusively from the child's point of view, letting go of the inclination to set the stage, which takes the reader out of the child's experience. We also suggested she write the story in the *present* tense. Here is the result.

WILLEM (2)

I am sitting in the grass. The grass is cool and green and very thick and soft; I sink in it. I like to sit there. The sun is very bright, but the hedge behind me makes a shade.

My brother is there, too. He is bigger than I. Papa and Mama are not there. I know they are in the house a little far away behind the hedge. But Willem is there. He is very big, almost as big as Papa. I like him. He always has something nice for me and my brother.

What will he do today? He is lying in the grass. There is also Joni. I do not know him too well, but he does not matter. Willem is there!

Willem is saying: *"Anak mau lihat Willem digiling sepeda?"* ("Kids, want to see the bike run over me?") Joni already goes to fetch the bicycle. There he comes—straight at Willem lying in the grass. Then the bicycle is already on the other side of Willem and Willem is standing up and laughing. He laughs at us kids. And then, with a laugh in his eye, he tells us, Papa's big truck will now run over his chest. Again he lies down in the thick grass— the car comes and it is over him—only his head sticks out—he is laughing at us. I hide my head. I am afraid and I grab my brother's hand. But I still look. Willem is already up again. Willem can do anything!!!

Years later when I talked about it, mother said, "Nonsense, he must have tricked you." But I still wonder, did it really happen?

◊ ◊ ◊

This rewrite of "Willem" is a much simpler story than the first version, isn't it? This version gives us the feeling of being "in" the event rather than watching it from a distance. In fact, we feel as if the event is happening to us, as if we are the child watching the truck go over Willem, wondering how such an awesome thing can happen.

Write in the present tense

Writing in the present tense gives the reader a wonderful sense of being present at or in the event. When we read a story written in the present tense, the events seem to be happening now; they seem to be happening around us rather than far away as if recollected through a tunnel. Little details suddenly become clearer and more vivid in our memories when we write in the present tense.

A child knows only what is directly in front of its eyes. Therefore, we believe a story written from the child's point of view more easily if it is written in the present tense. We may lose some information, but we gain a great deal in dramatic impact and in believability.

Writing in the present tense is not easy for some of us. We have been accustomed to writing in the past tense for so long we can hardly think of any other way. It also forces us to use our imagination a bit. However, one additional advantage is that when we write in the present tense it somehow puts our critic to rest for a while. We get out of our reflective, all knowing, critical adult selves and into a seeing, feeling, more innocent self.

Let's take another look at the garbage incident, now written in the present tense:

> I am twelve years old. Dad makes me take out garbage every day. Yuk. Everyday for six years. "When do I get a chance to do something important?" I wonder.

Suddenly, the story is more intimate, more vivid, more personal. This is a direction for us to explore.

If you can use the present tense, do so. If you are not comfortable doing so at first, keep writing your stories in the past tense. Then, from time to time, experiment with the present tense. Just change all the past tense verbs to present tense. "I walked" becomes "I walk" or "I am walking." Try it.

Write in the first person

Another difficulty for some of us is writing in the first person ("I was/am" rather than "he was/is" or "we were/are . . . "). Many of us were taught in school that it is self-centered to say "I." This makes it a bit difficult to write one's own life story.

In one of my classes, a tall, burly, ex-Marine named Joe Page begins reading:

> Joe P. got on his wagon and went down the hill really fast and then Joe P. nearly bumped a lady crossing the street. Joe rolled the wagon on its side. Joe really hurt himself.

"Joe," I say, after he has finished, "How long have you been out of the Marine Corps?"

He gazes at me for several seconds with those sad, tired eyes of his. " 'bout thirty five years," he answers in a soft voice.

I glance around the room. The fifteen other members of the class, all women, are very quiet. "Well, Joe," I reply, "It's OK to say 'I.' "

"You ever been in the service?" he asks, eyeing me closely. I nod. "Then you know." He pauses for a long moment. "When 'a first went in, 'bout 1926, my first sergeant, he says to me, 'You boys ain't people no more, you're part of the corps. It's 'we' and 'us' and 'the corps,' hear! I catch any you sayin' 'I' this or 'I' that, I'll bust your a____. So don't let me hear that d_____ word from any ya!!' "

"It's another time and another place, Joe," I say. "It's OK to say 'I.' Try it."

He nods, looking down at the page in front of him. "Mmm...mmm..." he stammers, wiping his face with a large red handkerchief. "Mmm got in the wagon and went down the hill." He glances up at me for an instant, then goes back to reading. "I got in my wagon and went down the hill," he mutters. His eyes meet mine for a moment, a hint of a grin comes to his mouth. "I nearly hit a lady and *I* turned my wagon over on its side ... and *I* fell out."

Joe looks at me, then at the others in the class. The silence turns into relaxed, amiable chatter. "I know just how you feel, Joe," says one lady, touching his sleeve. "I was raised the same way." Many of the others nod in agreement.

◊ ◊ ◊

An approach that works well if you have a group around you is to tell your earliest memory aloud, then tell it again, consistently using the present tense. Notice how you suddenly remember more of the incident. Then write down the incident on paper.

If you find yourself avoiding "I," perhaps by saying "*We* did such and such . . . ," remember: The days of your being unimportant are over. You are at the center of your autobiography. You may report what others are doing, but you are the person through whose eyes and ears we, the readers, experience the event. You are important. It is another time and place. It is OK to say "I."

If, at the *end* of this memory or subsequent early memories, you would like to add some background information and/or some of your present adult feelings about what happened back then, do so. But keep the adult reflection on the event distinct from the child's point of view. Jade's last line, "Years later when I talked about it, mother said . . . but I still wonder. . . " is a good example of including an adult reflection while keeping it distinct from the child's experience.

In successive stories we will continue to write from the child's point of view, although as we begin to write our more recent stories, we naturally know more of past and present and can set the stage more fully.

Please see Roz Belcher's story, "Goin' South" (page 177), as an example of a powerful memory seen from a child's point of view.

◊ ◊ ◊

Now that you have finished writing your earliest memory, you have done what every writer does: Compose, review, and rewrite. These are the same three steps you will follow with every story you write. As you write your earliest memories, you will find that even earlier incidents and experiences will return. The actual process of putting pen to paper seems to call up memories. Write these as soon as they become vivid and significant. Many life experiences block feelings, and writing unblocks these feelings and allows you to move ahead, free and unencumbered.

CHAPTER THREE

FINDING EARLY
VIVID MEMORIES

IT MAY BE HARD TO BELIEVE, BUT YOU ARE NOW A writer. You have written a memoir, received some response, rewritten it, and read it to your friends or relatives. In all probability they liked it. Of course, "one memoir does not a writer make," but be good to yourself. Accept the praise. And congratulations! Now you are ready to go on to the next memory or series of memories.

This may be a little more difficult. You've done a few scales and a simple tune; now we'll try you out on something harder. At the same time we will look for more places to improve your work during the reviewing phase and do more tinkering in the rewriting phase.

This time you are going to go back into the past in search of the earliest *vivid* memory you can find, a memory that stands out more than any other early memory. It may be an escape from a threatening situation when you were a child; it may be the death of a dear friend or relative; it may be a time in your life when you left or came to live at a special place; or it may be meeting a special person for the first time.

COMPOSING

Begin composing by following the six steps that were outlined in Chapter Two, directing your mind back toward your earliest vivid memory, one that truly stands out in high relief in your mind.

This early *vivid* memory should not be confused with your earliest memory, which may simply be a tiny fragment of recollection, like some archaeological relic from a prehistoric time. No, we are looking for an early memory that has power, a memory that is very strong.

Here are a number of "firsts" that may bring to mind some of the vivid moments of your life between, say, two and twelve years old:

— My most vivid memory of Mom or Dad

— My most embarrassing moment in school

— My first adventure

— My first time being really afraid

— My first success in school

— My most vivid recollection of Grandpa/Grandma

— My first kiss

— My first time getting into trouble

— My happiest time in school

— My best friend in school

◊ ◊ ◊

I am ready to return now to my storehouse of childhood memories. I am sitting in the right chair . . . the music may be playing . . . perhaps there is a fire in the fireplace . . . . I am ready to return to the time tunnel. Back I go . . . to a distant moment in time, keeping details in view, searching out lost ones . . . stripping away *the wrapping around my memories until I can see the moment clearly. I am ready to write **now**.*

◊ ◊ ◊

Write down everything you saw and experienced, at once. Don't stop, even if the pieces are disconnected. Don't stop, even if the memory makes you want to cry. If you begin crying, cry. But keep writing.

Now, how does the story read? Is it one story or fragments? Are the details sharper than in your first memoir? Are the feelings stronger? If you have written a series of fragments, would you like to fill in the gaps? If not, OK; go ahead and take this memoir to your group. Read it aloud and listen carefully to each response.

REVIEWING

During this second phase, we will learn more about what to look for when evaluating our own writing. I also want to talk about how to listen and offer helpful critiques when other people read their stories to us.

Let us begin with a checklist of the first steps in reviewing:

— resist the urge to change, to be too critical

— get feedback, go to a friend or group to get responses

— ask if the work is visual and emotion-producing

— listen to your own comments to see if something was left out

— express your stories as experiences seen from a child's point of view

Now let us go into some of these concerns a bit more thoroughly. Recalling the rewriting instructions of the previous chapter, we see that it is important to write visually and create emotional impact. You can enhance the visual clarity of the story by adding *detail*, by bringing the story closer to the reader with appropriate *dialogue,* by *focusing* on one incident at a time, and by *listening* carefully to feedback from the group and from yourself.

Detail

The first objective in writing good narrative stories is to make the events visible. The easiest way to do this is to bring the event into sharp focus by including little details which make the picture unique. Look at the following passage from "Uncle Eli" by Rose Rothenberg (the complete story is on page 198).

> Uncle Eli was a dapper man and extremely meticulous about his person. His shirts were always pure white, at least until they yellowed a bit with age. His dark serge suit was always well pressed and clean. It did not yellow with the passage of time, but took on a shine that competed with the gloss he maintained on his high-button shoes. In the summer months he sported spotless white buckskin oxfords—the same pair year after year. His straw hat was worn at a rakish angle and, rain or shine, he was never without an umbrella.

The details in this passage—the shirts "always pure white until they yellowed with age," the suit that "took on a shine," and the umbrella that was carried "rain or shine"— tell us a great deal about the man's character: his stubbornness, inflexibility, and pride in the face of changing circumstances.

Now let us look at another passage rich with details that reveal a great deal. This is taken from a longer story, a complete version of which appeared in the first edition of *Writing From Within.*

LIFE ON THE RAILROAD
by Eugene Mallory

The year was 1904. Not a good year for the overbuilt, midwestern railroads or the ever-distressed farmer either.

The Missouri Pacific Red Ball freight was two hours out on a night run west. The nearly new Baldwin 4-8-2, burning clean Colorado coal, was really showing what it could do.

Conductor William Sidel was riding the high seat in the cupola of the darkened caboose and pondering what he should do with his upside down life in general. First as a boomer brakeman, so called because he and many other bold young men had followed the railroad expansion of the late 1800s wherever the new rails led. Always moving on to new runs, new towns.

Then a bit of luck, and a bit of the old blarney, and he had his own train on the Hampton, Algona and Western, riding the varnish, not a crummy caboose. Even if the varnish was only an old combination coach; half seats, half mail and baggage, and his little conductor cubbyhole. The coach had to be there to satisfy the franchise, and he had trundled it up and down the 90 miles of lightweight rail that was all the Hampton, Algona and Western ever amounted to. No matter that many grand names had been painted over or that the old coach was hung on the end of an untidy string of freight cars and seldom exceeded 20 miles per hour, it was varnish.

A perfect old man's job, while he was still young, had perhaps made him old in too few years. God forbid!

But why was he uneasy on this perfect prairie night? True, when he had totaled his manifests, the weight of this train had shocked him, and now his certified reliable watch said they had covered 40 miles of track in the last hour. Things had changed while he had vegetated on the "branch" ....

◊ ◊ ◊

The phrase "riding the high seat in the cupola of the darkened caboose and pondering what he should do with his upside down life" gives us a vivid picture of a man perched up high, looking out on the moving train and looking inward on his life in the darkness. Another phrase, "no matter that many grand names had been painted over," gives us an equally vivid picture of time passing.

These phrases are good examples of the power of well-chosen details to convey information and feeling. What you will want to avoid is giving lots of details about objects when you are describing, say, a room or a place. Select details carefully, otherwise they can become repetitive and boring. The most interesting and useful details seem to be those which give a glimpse of *what* people do and *why* they do it.

Dialogue

Perhaps you have heard this comment about your stories from one of your classmates or friends: "It was a good story and the details were good, but I still didn't feel close to what was happening." If so, there is another technique which will help you bring the reader or listener closer to the action: dialogue. Not a lot. Just a little, in fact. Begin by trying to remember what your characters actually said way back when. If you can't quite remember what they said, write down what they might have said. As you do that, something inside of you will say, "Yes, that's close," or "No, that doesn't feel right at all." Improvising dialogue this way will carry you closer to what actually was said provided you *write*, not just *think*, the words you are seeking. In general, try to keep your dialogue to a sentence or two each time a character speaks. Here is an example of good dialogue, well remembered.

JEFFERSON BARRACKS, MISSOURI

by John Strong

We stepped outside for some fresh air. As luck would have it, the pigeon air corps was practicing dive bombing with Ford's new green sweater as target.

"Why did those damn pigeons pick on me?" lamented Ford, as he tried to wipe the droppings from his sweater with his handkerchief.

"Because they knew we were headed for the Air Corps and wanted to show us some expert bombing!" I joked.

"This isn't funny, John," protested Ford.

"Maybe they hate Irishmen and you're Irish and wearing green," I laughed.

"But you're Irish and a bigger target. Why didn't they pick on you?" asked Ford.

"Oh, can it, Ford," I yelled. "I'll give you the money to get it cleaned. This is trivial compared to the army life we've gotten into."

"Maybe Jefferson Barracks will be better," offered optimist Bill. But when we pulled into St. Louis next morning, Ford was still talking about the big stain on his sweater, the size of a pancake.

I went to a phone in the station, collecting my thoughts for my official call to Jefferson Barracks as the officer at Harrisburg had instructed.

"Sir, this is Recruit John Strong, with recruits Bill Bee and Ford Smith. We are coming from Harrisburg, Pennsylvania. I have all the necessary papers," I recited in a good strong voice, trying to make a favorable impression.

On the other end of the line, I heard a child-like voice squealing, "What son of a bitch stole my comic book? It was a Dick Tracy one, too. Come on, cough it up." Then he grumbled to me, "Say that again," which I did.

His next words really startled me. "What the hell do you expect me to do about it?" I thought I had a captain's young son on the phone, so I remained silent for a moment. "You got a tongue, ain't you? Now tell me what you want me to do," the brat ranted. "I have no papers on you at all."

"Maybe you can suggest how we can get to Jefferson Barracks," I offered, with a slight sneer in my voice.

"No one told me you were coming. The only way you can get here is in the mail truck. It's due at the station in about fifteen minutes, so get your asses to the entrance or you will have to walk the fifteen miles to get here. If you don't get here by midnight, you will be A.W.O.L." With that, the jerk slammed the phone down.

◊ ◊ ◊

Notice that new characters are introduced quickly through dialogue: "I heard a child-like voice squealing, 'What son of a bitch stole my comic book?' " Soon we learn this is his new commanding officer—a quick, unexpected glimpse of a new character. This is good dialogue at work.

Note: When writing dialogue, put the "he said" or "she said" (or "replied," etc.) *after* the dialogue—"Come home," Mother said—or in the *middle* of the dialogue, after the first phrase if possible: "Come home right now," Mother said, "and don't go out again before dark."

Avoid placing the "he said" or "she said" at the beginning of the phrase or sentence—Mother said, "Come home." There is more surprise for us if we hear the dialogue for a moment before we learn who said it. But be sure we know who is speaking shortly after that person begins to speak.

Focus

A vivid memory may in fact be a *series* of vivid memories, so you must develop a sense of where the episode begins and ends, and write only *one* episode at a time. This is called focus. Classically, in an Ibsen play for example, a play begins only after some important event has taken place—a death, a crime, etc. In your work you may start with a similar event, or just before the event. What is important is to get the reactions of the major characters throughout the episode and to know when the incident or event ends.

Focus is also related to finding the "spine", which we will discuss in greater detail in Chapter Five under "Form and Structure." For a good example of a well-focused story that incorporates a series of powerful memories, see Edith Ehrenreich's "The *Anschluss* of Austria" on page 191.

Focusing on what the episode is about—where it begins and ends—and writing visually using details make up what we call narrative or storytelling. Ultimately, you will be seeking a balance between narration, dialogue, and your inner thoughts and feelings.

Tips on listening effectively and giving concise feedback

Listening constructively to the stories other writers are telling can help us develop objectivity about our own work. It also helps to develop a rapport with the other writers, who might welcome our feedback, and is a source of new ideas.

The first rule in "reviewing" others' work is: Proceed with caution. Our biggest problem as listeners is that we want to be right—and righteous. We want to be able to make the smartest comment, and we want to say nothing that will expose us to criticism.

If we say too much, we will sound critical and may discourage the writer with our negativity. If we say too little—"I liked it," "That was very nice"—we may give him or her nothing to work with, or may give a false sense of effectiveness.

Begin by paying close attention to your feelings. Ask yourself, How do I feel after listening to this story? Does it touch my emotions? Does it make me happy or sad, carefree or thoughtful? Then tell the writer what your feelings are.

Is the story memorable? Could you see everything? Were there plenty of vivid, fresh details throughout? Can you remember them? Let the writer know just how visual his or her story is.

If you are the writer, note carefully how you respond and what you say when class members comment on your story. Try not to defend yourself. Just explain, if you feel you need to, what was behind some of the creative decisions you made. And as I've already said, listen to yourself. What you say to your friends after you have read the story aloud may provide valuable information, which you may have excluded in your first draft. Often a classmate will ask a provocative question, one which you, the writer, would like to have asked yourself in the first place. Writers frequently answer questions offhandedly, only to realize they have revealed important information or details that would flesh out the story. So, as a writer, listen to what you say during these question-and-answer periods.

Follow these suggestions and you will find your group discussions becoming more and more helpful as well as interesting.

I talk at length about supportive feedback in Chapter Seven. This is a very important element in your writing process, and it deserves careful attention. If you are already working in a writing group, you may want to skip ahead and review that chapter before you go on.

REWRITING

You are now ready to begin rewriting your second story. You have a greater fund of techniques at your disposal and a more thorough grasp of what these techniques can do. You have the responses of your friends or classmates to help you. Likewise, you have a better grasp of how to look at your own work after writing that first draft.

We tend to think of rewriting as very taxing, perhaps boring, maybe even painful. But the results are almost always worth the effort. To have one's work go straight through to the mind and heart of the reader feels wonderful, as you are no doubt finding out. At this point, review the steps we discussed in rewriting your first memoir—

— write visually

— include your feelings to create emotional impact

— write from a child's point of view if your stories are about childhood

— use the present tense

— write from the first person

— and add to them the concerns we have just mentioned in our review phase: details, dialogue, and focus. Do not try to rewrite on a step-by-step basis, however. Once you have given thought to these various areas of improvement, read your story over and make gut-level changes where it feels right to do so.

Having done your rewriting, take your story back to your friends, relatives, and classmates. I think you will be pleasantly surprised. And if you want to write several more "vivid memories" before going on to the next chapter, do so.

CHAPTER FOUR

DESCRIBING
INTERESTING PEOPLE

Unlike the Lilliputians in *Gulliver's Travels*, into whose world a big person was suddenly cast, we are all born into a world of big people. Mothers and fathers, in particular, loom especially large in our lives and in our imaginations. Sometimes they appear distorted. My father, for example, appeared to most people as a strong-minded, humorous, thin-skinned, and occasionally imperious man. To me, as I was growing up, he appeared so powerful that, until well into my thirties, I had dreams in which he appeared as a pursuing monster and I was a frightened Lilliputian.

Family members, many of whom have great power over us, must be dealt with in our memories honestly, clear-sightedly, and fearlessly. Since our view of them changes as we grow older, it is both appropriate and necessary to see them as they were experienced by other members of the family and by ourselves at different times in our lives.

COMPOSING

Let's consider what makes a character in a book, a play, or a movie "interesting," and see how it applies to our parents and the rest of the family. We might begin with the following definition: An interesting person is someone who wants something badly (*what* he wants is usually very clear) and takes an interesting, unusual, or difficult route to reach that goal (*how* he is going to get it is also clear). To the degree that the goal is dangerous and the means employed involve risk, the person might move up the scale from interesting to heroic.

Character qualities

How a person goes about getting what he or she wants reveals certain character qualities. Charm, determination, humor, honesty, self-assurance, dependability, opportunism, perfectionism are all qualities which get us what we want; they may also, tragically, defeat us in other ways.

At this point I would like you to read two stories. The first one, which we've already discussed, is "Uncle Eli" by Rose Rothenberg (page 198), and the question is, can you tell what the central character, Uncle Eli, wants? The second story, "Escape to Freedom" by Rose Saposnek (page 181), is about a mother bringing her daughter out of Russia during the pogroms of the Russian Revolution of 1917. Determining what she wants is not difficult, but see if you can identify her character qualities. In both stories, try to figure out what incidents reveal how interesting and/or heroic these people are.

After you have had a chance to read about and discuss several kinds of interesting characters, take some time to write about one yourself. Follow these five steps:

1. Think of a character you consider interesting.

2. Recall an incident, event, or series of actions that were typical of this character.

3. Find a word for the memorable quality or qualities he or she possesses.

4. Ask yourself if the incident you recalled really brings out the quality you have identified. If it does, then go ahead and write about it; if not, then you may wish to select a different incident.

5. Remember that the most interesting characters have several strong qualities, sometimes contradictory ones.

Here are some possible interesting or important people about whom you can write:

— My grandparents

— My parents

— My sister(s) or brother(s)

— My best friend from the time I was __ years old

— My first teacher, mentor, or guide

— My first boss

— My "black sheep" relative

— My companion through a difficult ordeal

◊ ◊ ◊

I lean back in my chair. The images of the past rise up to meet me through the murky depths to the present. The place and person become clearer. I begin to write now.

REVIEWING

In reviewing our stories, we want to continue to add to our techniques and concerns, so we will now address two additional aspects of writing: setting the stage, and finding emotion in the facts.

Setting the stage

When a story begins, a number of questions arise in the reader or listener almost immediately: What is going to happen, who is doing what to whom, why is it happening, and where is it taking place? A good story will address all of these questions soon after the curtain goes up, and it will answer most of them by the time the curtain descends. "Setting the stage" answers the questions, "Where are we?" "From what position or angle are we viewing the action?" and "What information do we need to know in order to understand what is happening?"

Exactly where a writer or an artist positions us will have a powerful influence on the meaning of the story or incident we are viewing. This may be easier to understand with a painting, so let us look at two examples. The first is Leonardo da Vinci's "The Last Supper."

We are placed directly in front of Christ, able to see the effects, on either side of him, of his statement, "One of you shall betray me." We are neither below nor above the action, neither awed by nor superior to it. It is happening directly in front of us, in a clearly defined space in which a fifteenth-century Tuscan valley unfolds behind the head of Christ. We know where we are, and from what position we are seeing the action. It is "real" to us.

Another interesting example is Peter Brueghel's "The Fall of Icarus." Here we are placed high on a hill overlooking a distant harbor in a place that resembles northern Europe. It is early in the sixteenth century.

We are placed near a peasant whose chores will take him down and to the left in the painting. Our eye is led to the distant vistas: to the new "round" world beyond. Because of our position near the peasant, we would most likely ignore anything in the lower right portion of the painting, such as the leg of Icarus, who has just fallen out of the sky. (You may recall that Icarus and Daedalus escaped from the labyrinth of King Minos by making wings of wax. Though advised by his father not to fly too close to the sun, Icarus disobeyed and plunged into the sea when his wings melted.)

What is the meaning of this painting? Perhaps something like, "We are all so preoccupied with our daily tasks, we hardly see the truly important events in life taking place. We are distracted by the boring necessities of life (the peasant's tasks) and the world's concerns (opening up the world and viewing it, not as flat, but as round)."

The settings of these paintings and the perspectives from which we view the action have a great deal of influence on their message and impact on us, and it is similar with stories. For examples of how a story can be framed or introduced, please look at Lucy Mac-Dougall's "Some Days the Bird Sings" in Chapter Thirteen (and other stories in Part III).

We can see quite vividly the setting and surroundings in which the story happens. This is the key: to be able to see the surroundings as clearly as if they had been photographed.

In fact, the techniques I am suggesting are cinematic ones. Many modern films begin with a tight shot, then widen to include everything important, so your establishing shot might come after a line or two of dialogue or some action at the beginning of the story. This is the way Lucy's story unfolds. I often advise my students to begin with action or dialogue to get the reader into the story quickly, then set the stage in the second paragraph.

Another technique, which early film makers often used, is this sequence: first, the establishing shot, a wide-angle shot encompassing a whole city or village; next, a medium shot bringing us closer to the particular dwellings or places we are going to inhabit, and finally, a closer shot of the characters important to this narrative.

If you are writing stories of your life when you were less than ten years old, that is, writing from a child's point of view, establishing shots might actually be unbelievable at the beginning of a story. The child's world is a very tiny and narrow, though fascinating, one. So an establishing shot—a more comprehensive, adult view—might come at the *end* of the scene or story. After the story ends, you may also wish to tell the reader how the event described has affected you over the ensuing years.

Setting the stage is related to writing from a child's point of view in this way: As a young child, I see the world through a very small window. I know little of what others are doing. I know nothing of past and future. It is a very particular stage setting. As I mature, the window through which I see the world widens. I know more of past and present, of life beyond myself; therefore, I can set the stage more fully.

As a writer, I ask my reader to suspend his or her normal disbelief and believe what I have written. From a child, the reader can only believe the world as seen through the tiny window of a small child's awareness, but from a more mature youngster or an adult the reader can accept a much more fully set stage.

Remember, when setting the stage, that describing a setting is not necessarily a matter of inspiration. One need not go into a creative trance in order to create a solidly visual picture. In fact, the beginning of the story can be lightly sketched in at first, and the details of time and place filled in later, when the story is about to be completed. Do not get bogged down in details of time and place when you are first setting down your narrative.

Finding emotion in the facts

By now you've had a chance to listen to narratives from the other members of your group. Have you noticed that some of the stories or incidents really stir up emotions in you, while others, though they may be descriptive and have good dialogue, just don't do anything? Perhaps your narrative is one of these. You may be defending yourself, saying, "That's how I remember things," but still, something is missing. Well, there are ways of getting more feeling into your writing, ways that will cause readers or members of your group to remember your story and say, "Now that really stirred me up."

We have talked about the difference between the right and left brains. Are you aware that there are also different "eyes" with which to see? Yes, that's what I said, different eyes.

Oh, I know we have two eyes which are plainly visible to everyone, eyes on either side of our nose, eyes which look out on the world and tell us how it is. Some anthropologists and paleophysiologists, however, believe there is evidence of an ancient "third" eye located in the middle of the forehead: the eye of the Cyclops. This third eye may or may not actually exist, but what is important is that, symbolically, this third eye is the eye of self-awareness, the eye of the inner world. In particular, it is the eye of knowing how we *feel* as we watch, observe, and participate in the experiences of the outside world. Using our third eye, we can record our feelings and reactions to events as they go by.

This would be a good time to read a passage which

reveals what the writer is *feeling* as well as seeing in her mind's eye as she writes about a person in her life.

A LOST SOUL

by Rose Rothenberg

I see Kate as she was then in the bloom of her youth, yet so oddly old beyond her years. Her lustrous, red, wavy hair was worn shoulder length, parted on the side, brushed away from her rather plain face and held in place with a barrette. Stylish tortoiseshell glasses failed to hide the pain reflected in her pale brown eyes. A sprinkling of freckles spotted her forehead and extended into the areas just under the eyes.

Kate was a pleasant, soft-spoken, agreeable girl, but often seemed distant, as if only a part of her were involved with the present. Quite often, too, when her features relaxed in a lovely, wide-mouthed smile, her eyes remained sad, remote.

The sadness I perceived in her spoke to a certain melancholy of my own spirit that surfaced now and then, and I was drawn to her.

◊ ◊ ◊

In these paragraphs, we can find numerous phrases which evoke emotions about the person being described: "bloom of her youth . . . oddly old . . . glasses failed to hide the pain reflected in her pale brown eyes," and finally, "her features relaxed in a lovely, wide-mouthed smile, [but] her eyes remained sad, remote." We also get a picture of the writer's feelings in the last sentence.

So we can see that with this third eye, the eye of intuition or awareness, we not only detect a certain sadness in her friend, we also notice how our *own* sadness is touched by hers. The emotion in the object of the description, Kate, is echoed by the emotion in the writer, Rose, and this is clearly communicated to us. In this way we find emotion in the facts.

REWRITING

Many of you may be feeling that rewriting is still beyond you, that it takes time and you are not sure what the benefits will be. You may also be asking, "How can an experienced writer like Bernard Selling know how I feel about rewriting?" Virtually all writers go through a rewriting process that involves considerable change. Many of us write first drafts that are undistinguished and uninteresting. What counts is what we do after we have gotten through the first draft.

So that you can see what I myself go through, I am going to write about an interesting character using the techniques I have given you so far. What you are about to read is exactly what comes from my head and my typewriter. Will it be any good? Will it be interesting? I have no idea. I will follow the steps I outlined for you and see where they lead.

1. "Think of a character you consider interesting."
   My father...

2. "Recall an incident, event, or series of actions that were typical of this character."
   Hmm... I'm not ready for that...

3. "Find a word for the memorable quality or qualities he possesses."
   His curiosity... his desire to know... but the way he died? Ah, there's the incident... his death... what kind of curiosity could kill him ... uh, hmm... pickiness, his insatiable desire to pick at the surface of things. That's it!! His intellectual curiosity and the way he died, together.

DAD'S DEATH

by Bernard Selling

FIRST DRAFT

My father had an insatiable desire to pick away at the surface of things. Intellectually, it caused him to be unendingly curious, devouring books, thoughts, and concepts hungrily. He loved learning and absorbing and analyzing, acquiring two Ph.D.s and an M.D. As director of the Recorder's Court Psychopathic Clinic, he was an innovator in the field of traffic offenses, alcoholism, and emotional disorders. Yet this insatiable desire to pick away at the surface of things had another outcome.

In the winter of 1955, he found a wart on his foot, a wart that bothered him. He picked up a razor blade from his shaving kit and began to pick away at the wart. The razor was dirty and infected. By the end of the month he had blood poisoning and was hospitalized. Shortly after, under the threat of having his leg amputated, he got up in the middle of the night, slipped, broke his hip, had a heart attack, and died. My mother and sister and I could hardly believe what had happened.

◊ ◊ ◊

Now I've finished this first draft and I look it over. I realize I'm not in the picture, nor are my feelings. I begin to look for me in the picture to see where I am and how I'm feeling. I go back to the time he was in the hospital and see how I feel. I begin to write:

I am sixteen and bewildered. "How can he have done this?" I wonder. He is smart. He has two Ph.D.s and an M.D.

I think back to how I feel after his death. "I am so angry at him for dying. I can almost burst."

Why? I wonder. "He and I have been battling with each other," I answer myself. "Only recently does he even begin to know who I am, sort of." Am I only angry? "I miss him," I write. "The funeral is a blur."

◊ ◊ ◊

I review the story again. Yes, I'm in the story and so are my feelings, but the whole thing sounds rather academic and feels kind of remote. "How can I put this in a book on writing?" my critic asks. "It's OK," my creator answers. "I'm letting them see how I get past the first draft."

If this were one of my students writing, what would I suggest he or she do at this point? "Find out where the story begins." So I look over the draft again. Ah, there it is: "In the winter of 1955, he finds a wart on his foot." Maybe it's going to be a different sort of story, I say to myself. "Go on, make changes, see what happens—and try it in the present tense."

SECOND DRAFT

One day, Dad finds a wart on the bottom of his foot. It is winter, 1955. He is fifty-three years old and not too well. He coughs a lot during the winter. I know he had a heart attack eight years ago. I worry about him. We all do. With a razor blade from his shaving kit, he begins to pick away at his wart. Nobody tells him not to. Nobody can tell him anything. A month later he has blood poisoning and is hospitalized. Shortly after, he is told that he may have to have his leg amputated. I am sixteen and bewildered. "How can he have done this?" I ask. "He is smart. He has two Ph.D.s and an M.D. His brain cuts through stupidity, error, nonsense, and people's bullshit all the time. I'm afraid he'll cut through mine sometime."

Mom and Lee, my fourteen-year-old sister, go to see him in the hospital. I don't. It's Saturday and I play tennis with the guys instead. Afterwards, Lee tells me that Mom and Dad were like young lovers.

"He was telling all his old dirty jokes," she says, "and Mom was laughing and giggling like a school-girl. It was so . . . erotic, you could cut it with a knife."

I nod, feeling numb, wondering what I have missed.

Sometime after New Year's, he is still in the hospital. The doctors want to operate. He's out-raged, I'm told later by my mother. He gets up in the middle of the night, slips, breaks his hip, and . . .

No, that's not quite how it is. I look back to see where I have gone off . . . Ah, last paragraph.

Sometime after New Year's Day, I am in my room. I am working on a model train. The phone rings upstairs somewhere. I hear Mom answer it. A few moments later she comes into my room.

"Lopo (Lowell) died this morning," she says quietly. "He got up in the middle of the night. He was angry at the doctors. He slipped, broke his hip, and had a heart attack."

I listen. I walk away—or does she? We say nothing to one another.

I go to school the next day. Everyone knows he is dead. His picture is on the front page of the Orlando paper. I can see they are shocked that I'm here in school.

Finally, Bill Bledsoe comes up to me. "I'm sorry to hear what happened," he says. "I liked your dad." I mumble something. Later in the day, Bill Nichols comes up and says the same thing. No one else says anything about my father. Friends say nothing. Teachers say nothing. Mom says nothing.

Dad is dead. No more arguments. No more fights. No more misunderstandings. No more laughter. Would he have forgiven me for my breaking his prized Spike Jones records in a fit of anger if he had lived? Could I have found out why he got so furious at me for holding hands with Jeri B. when I was thirteen and staying out in the canoe with Pat C. when I was fourteen?

I was so angry at him, so humiliated, I would have loved to have knocked him down but, no, I couldn't. He might have died. So many questions, so many feelings haunt me. Why this? Why that? I am so angry at him I can hardly see straight. The funeral is a blur.

The rest of the year I go inside myself.

"Do you want to play the lead in 'Dangerous Dan McGrew'?" the band master asks me. It's the part in the band skit that had the audiences howling when I played it the year before. Dad was laughing so hard that even from the stage I could see him wiping the tears from his eyes.

"No," I answer. I play in the band. I get decent grades. I go through the motions. I don't want to be noticed, and no one does. Dad is dead and part of me is too.

Now, looking back, going through the feelings again, I find it hard to believe that Dad would place himself in such a vulnerable position—a man with diabetes and a history of heart disease, a doctor and a man of science, a man with a family he cared about so deeply, picking at a wart on the bottom of his foot with a dirty razor blade. That insatiable desire to pick away at things got him.

◊ ◊ ◊

Keeping a checklist

As we review and rewrite, we need to keep in mind all of the things we learned earlier, while adding new items to the "stew." In fact, we might want to make a checklist of questions to ask ourselves, as do pilots, who go through a list of procedures before take-off and landing. The checklist might look like this:

---

1. Is my story visual?

2. Does it have emotional impact?

3. Is it told from a consistent point of view? A child's perhaps? Is it told in the present tense and the first person?

4. Do the details make the story clearer and more interesting?

5. Does the dialogue help tell the story and make the characters more interesting?

6. Have I kept to one well-focused incident at a time?

7. Are the characters' "qualities" evident?

8. Have I set the stage, giving some background and context?

9. Are my feeling about the events clearly expressed?

Rewriting now becomes easier because you know what has to be done and you have a variety of techniques with which to approach the task. At this point, look over your checklist, begin to visualize any changes you may wish to make, then make them.

CHAPTER FIVE

REVISING AND REVISIONING YOUR WORK

Y OUR PAST IS LIKE A REFRIGERATOR," I OFTEN TELL my students. "Once the door is open, write the memories that are directly in front of you, the most vivid ones, the ones that press themselves upon you. When you've finished with those, others in the back will come forward."

"Suppose I can't get the door open," a student may reply. "What do I do?"

One key to unlocking the door is to concentrate on a place where vital, unforgettable things happened.

COMPOSING

Describing a Place Memory

Here is a process which may help you pry that door open. First, imagine yourself floating over that place of significance. Next, ask yourself, "What sorts of things did I do there?" Then try answering your questions with *-ing* words, action words. "I found myself *exploring* the house ... *wandering* the woods." Finally, allow the *-ing* words you have written down to help you find specific, vivid moments about which to write.

Try to find memories from your childhood first. You can begin by describing a place which generated experiences affecting you or members of your family.

One such vital and unforgettable place for me is the farmhouse my sister and I have up in Maine. My father bought it for my mother during the depression. Restoring it was their life's project. I spent almost every summer there from the time I was six months old until I was eighteen. Even now I return almost every summer.

As I imagine floating over the house, a flood of memories comes back to me: *watching* Abner haying with his two-horse team, *reading* by a kerosene lamp at night, *exploring* our pre-Revolutionary War farmhouse, *celebrating* V-J Day near a lake where the ties of a forgotten railroad lay underfoot, *forming* my first band to play at church suppers, *holding* hands for the first time in the picture show, *seeing* Mom and Dad happy together in a way they never were in Florida, *taking* my wife and infant son to Maine and *creating* our second child on the dock at Songo Pond, *filming* my sons *exploring* the old railroad, *working* side by side with the boys for more than ten summers to clear the brush that had overgrown the meadows during my neglectful years.

As an example of a well-described place memory, please see Gene Mallory's "Houses" in Chapter Six. Grace Holcomb/Ted Brown's story "Pool Hall," excerpted in Chapter Seventeen, is also good.

In Gene's story the writer's real concern is what has happened and what will happen in this vividly remembered place. Yes, the mood, atmosphere, and detail of the place are important, but it is the movement of things and people in and around this place that will make your story memorable.

Here are some places which may contain significant, vivid memories:

— Places where I lived as a child

— Places where I played as a child

— Places where I did something I shouldn't have done

— Places where I learned a lesson I have never forgotten

— Places where I saw (or experienced) things that changed my life

— The place where Dad did his work

— The place where Grandpa or Grandma lived when I was small

— The place where I had my first kiss

— The place where I worked for the first time

As we wander back through the years remembering the things we have done, particular moments from our past begin to reappear. The door of the refrigerator has swung open and we see that the top shelf is full.

"But maybe I don't want to remember," you say. "My past was full of pain and I only want to get to the happy things."

The more deeply we write from within ourselves, the more fully we can capture an experience that may have been haunting us, find its meaning, then let go of it. This clears such memories, both positive and negative ones, from the front of our minds and allows us to explore previously hidden but no less intriguing and vivid memories.

◊ ◊ ◊

*I'm getting ready to write what happened to me in a place of importance. I'm not going to get bogged down in details of the place ... I'm ready to go back ... way back ... I'm going back to a vivid event in a special place ... I'm going to begin writing **now**.*

REVIEWING

As we come to the reviewing phase of our work, we will add two other elements to our checklist:

— Improvising with the facts when memory fails

— A concern for form and structure: finding the spine of the story

Improvising: Filling in the gaps where memory fails

As you continually dig up and confront your memories, you may begin to feel like something of an archaeologist. The brain is a magnificent and fascinating organ, fascinating because it often yields up what it wishes to give us, not what we think it ought to be giving us. Within its rich bank of memories you have undoubtedly discovered several fragments of recollections which seem to form a whole, but somehow you cannot complete it—the names, places, and times that are the links between the fragments appear to be lost. As a result, you may feel stuck and unable to write or complete a memoir.

The experienced archaeologist not only knows where to dig for artifacts of the past, but, when they are in hand, he also knows how to put them together in such a way that he can make educated guesses about ancient habits, customs, and beliefs. The past becomes clearer.

So, what does one do if one simply doesn't have enough evidence to create the links to complete the story that is lurking inside one's brain? Frustrating, isn't it? A paradox—to know that one's most interesting memory is the story one doesn't remember.

This is where we must operate not as a scientist but as an artist, not as an archaeologist but as a lover, in fact, as more than a lover.

Picasso once said, "Art is a lie that tells us the truth," and this is the sense in which we must become artist, lover, seducer, and Casanova. As a lure to bringing out the truth we must be willing to invent, to lie a little. Oh, not to ourselves, or even to our readers, but definitely to our brain. Invention is a creative right-brain strategy that we sometimes need to get past the guard of our critical left brain, which, for reasons of its own, is trying to hide the past.

So, as you move from the terra firma of one clear-as-a-bell memory to another equally well-grounded memory, if you suddenly find yourself sinking into the quicksand of no memory, you can regain your footing by simply *inventing* parts of an episode until the clear memory reappears.

Perhaps you don't like the idea of lying; perhaps this suggestion arouses in you the same enthusiasm that you had for castor oil as a child and curfews as a teenager. "I'm not a person who invents," a student will often protest. "If I wanted to write fiction, I would write fiction. I'm here to write my life's stories." This is all quite true. But we are not dropping invented artifacts into archaeological digs and trying to pretend they are real—a Piltdown Man approach to life story writing. Not at all.

Our purpose is to entice the brain into yielding up the truth. So, once we have invented part of the story, we must rely on our intuition to let us know when something feels false, and then rewrite it, moving toward the truth as best we can.

Occasionally, the brain does not yield what we

hope it will. In that case, simply preface the passage with a phrase such as, "As well as I can remember..." or, "My memory is a bit blank here, but I think the next part of the story goes something like this...." A disclaimer like that is all you need. No one can then hold you to the facts; you are off the hook. If a question which you cannot answer arises in your mind, by all means deal with the question and answer it by saying "I don't remember" or "I don't know." If the question comes up, it is integral to the story and *must* be answered, even if the answer is simply, "I don't remember." This way the reader will not remain puzzling over the question and be distracted from the rest of the story.

Here are some simple guidelines for improvising:

First, when facts are available, stick to the facts you know to be true. Do not invent facts just to make a better sounding story. If you do, people will come to mistrust you and will cease believing your stories.

Second, allow yourself to re-create and improvise your own feelings. The reader wants to know what is going on inside you. Do not suppose what other's feelings are unless you can read the expressions on their faces, hear what they are saying, or read their body language. If you try to tell the reader what other people are feeling inside, your reader will not believe you.

Third, allow yourself to re-create dialogue using the truth of your intuition and feelings as a guide to what is believable. Readers crave dialogue as an alternative to narrative and inner thoughts and feelings.

And *finally,* if the facts as you remember them simply do not feel real somehow, then write what *feels* real and add a postscript explaining the difference.

Form and structure (1): Finding the spine

Form is a tricky thing to talk about with writers. It is one of those things that all writers and writing teachers love to discuss. Knowledge of form is what makes a writer an expert, just as being able to fill cavities is what makes a dentist an expert. Or at least that is what writers like to believe.

Essentially, form gives one's work some definable shape, so that the readers or listeners may know where they are going and can enjoy where they have been. A story about a duck needs to be about a duck. A story about an abortion needs to be about an abortion. A story about an uncle needs to be about an uncle. As a writer, this involves giving the reader or listener little clues about what to look for or listen for, a coherent thread, or even a running gag.

Sometimes a mood or an atmosphere running through a story can also provide form. Stories can hang heavy with memory and emotion. This, too, is form.

Each story has its own emotional logic, its own concerns, and the line of that logic is the "spine." Anything else should be left aside, or saved for another story. Other concerns, issues, and people, need to be dealt with at a later time. Finding and then keeping to the spine is closely related to structure. Since the mind can hold just so many things in it at one time, we have to limit the mind's attention to those things that are related to the spine.

Let's suppose, for example, the beginning of our first draft is about taking a trip from Russia to the U.S.A., the middle is about finding a house to settle in so that Mom, who is sick, can feel better, and the end of the story is about Mom's death and how everyone felt.

From the ending, we get a clue about the spine and the structure. In fact, the middle—Mom's getting sick—is also a clue. The beginning needs to relate to the end, so the beginning of the story needs to be about Mom's health or well-being. The trip from Russia is clearly a separate story.

Here is what our review checklist might look like now:

---

1. Is my story visual?

2. Does it have emotional impact?

3. Is it told from a consistent point of view? Am I writing in the first person and the present tense?

4. Do the details make the story clearer and more interesting?

5. Does the dialogue help tell the story and make the characters more interesting?

6. Have I kept to one well-focused incident at a time?

7. Are the characters' qualities evident?

8. Have I set the stage properly: Have I created a window through which the action can be seen, and possibly given a little background?

9. Are my feelings about the incident clearly expressed?

10. Have I improvised toward the facts where my memory has failed?

11. Does my story have a spine to it?

REWRITING

For those of you who are continually working on rewriting your stories to make them more interesting and more readable, other ways your story can be rewritten to make it tighter and more effective are to find the beginning of your story and to expand the climax of your story.

Form and structure (2): Finding the beginning of your story

Here are a few simple steps to follow to find the beginning of your story.

First, ask yourself, "What is the most powerful moment of this vivid memory of mine? What is the moment I remember most clearly?" Then ask yourself, "Can I start my story *just before* this vivid moment begins?" Usually, as writers, we give much more introductory information than the reader needs to know, information which can be left out or rearranged.

Then, after you have finished your first draft, look over your story right away. Find that first line of dialogue or action. Often, the closer we get to the more vividly recalled moments in the story, the more dialogue we will naturally write. That first line of dialogue may be a clue to the beginning of the story and to the spine of the story as well.

Don't worry about starting off the story with a perfect opening when you are writing your first draft. Finding the beginning is strictly a *rewriting* task.

All artists need to warm up. Musicians do scales, actors do vocal and facial exercises, dancers stretch. Writers have to warm up, too, and that's what the first few paragraphs of each draft are—a warm-up . . . until you rewrite them. The first line of dialogue or action is where you begin to hit your stride. By that time you are in the story and so are we, your readers.

Now, please see "The Goose Story" by Vera Mellus as an example of rewriting by locating the first line of dialogue and by rearranging other paragraphs.

The Goose Story (1)

by Vera Mellus

1 {It was autumn. The leaves were turning red and yellow and it was a perfect day to take two little boys to the Los Angeles Zoo. I'm not familiar with the Zoo now, but then there was a barnyard where little children could pet goats and ponies, feed chickens, ducks and geese. They could also see a cow being milked.

My daughter and I packed a picnic basket and set off with two eager little boys. We strolled by the bears, tigers and other animals, but it wasn't till we got to the barnyard that the boys really became interested and had fun. Here they could come in close contact with the animals.

It was a perfect place to take pictures. How great to snap the children feeding chickens and to get those happy smiles on their faces.} {I was so

2 busy taking pictures I didn't notice a big, fat goose following me around.

I suddenly felt a hurtful pull and looked to see the goose had a tight grip on my big toe. He had braced his feet, stretched his neck to the last inch, and was hanging on.}

3 {"I can't believe this," I yelled. "Look, Dede."}

"Mother, give him a kick," I heard her yell, as she was having a fit of laughter.

"I can't. He won't let go."

"I'll get a stick," I heard my grandson say.

By this time we were all laughing so hard watching this silly goose.

A few days prior I had fallen in the shower and had broken the toes on my left foot. They were so swollen I couldn't wear a shoe and so was wearing sandals; one toe was so swollen it was white, and to a goose it must have looked like a fat, juicy grub.

He finally gave up seeing whether it was going to come off and I went home with all toes intact.

◊ ◊ ◊

Class members suggested she look at the first line of dialogue or action to see if that is where the spine of the story begins. Here is her second version.

THE GOOSE STORY (2)

2,
3

{"Oh, no. I can't believe this," I yell, shaking my foot, trying to discourage a big fat goose from trying to eat one of my toes. "Get away."}

1

{My daughter, her two sons, and I are in the barnyard of the Los Angeles Zoo. The boys are feeding the ducks and chickens and having a great time. I've been so busy trying to get those happy smiles with my camera that I haven't noticed this goose.}

"Get away. Shoo," I yell.

"Mother, kick him," I hear my daughter say, having a fit of laughter.

"I can't. He won't let go."

"I'll get a stick," my grandson says. "I'll make him let go."

By this time we are all laughing so hard to see this silly goose back up, brace himself, stretch his neck to the last inch and hang on.

I had fallen in the shower and the toes on my left foot are broken. I cannot wear a shoe and so I'm wearing sandals—and one toe is so swollen it is white and must look like a fat, juicy grub.

I brace myself and pull hard. He lets go. I limp away, then turn around. I'll never forget the look on his face. He stared at me—a look of triumph all over his face.

My two grandsons had a great day, but what really made the day was the goose.

◊ ◊ ◊

Notice that the spine of the story is now very apparent: the duck's attack on Vera and the comedy that ensues. In version 1 we had no idea what the story was about until we got to "2". In version 2, Vera drops much of "1", and combines "2" and "3"—dialogue and the spine begin together. Notice also that she has changed past tense verbs into present tense verbs.

Form and structure (3): Expanding the climax of your story

"I wanted to know more of what was happening at the climax of your story," a listener said to one student, Ed Boyle, after Ed had read the first draft of "Typhoon of Forty-Five." "It was so interesting I just wanted more."

I realized that several writers were getting that same kind of feedback, so I began suggesting that they expand the dramatic moment when everything is coming to a head.

In films, for example, a dramatic moment of action or feeling may actually be done in slow motion or repeated in slow motion, from several angles. In one of the more memorable scenes from the movie *A Man and a Woman* by Claude LeLouche, the camera circles the two lovers as they fall into each other's arms in the train station, as if spinning a web around them, sealing them off from the world outside, slowing down everything so it seems these passionate moments exist out of time. Such cinematic techniques allow the reader/listener/viewer to understand and savor every fraction of a moment of this wonderful experience. Similarly, baseball players, when they are hot, describe the ball coming to the plate as "large as a basketball and moving slowly... easy to hit." Everything is slowed down and the moment when bat strikes ball is expanded.

This is not to say that you, as writer, are trying to slow down the action. Including more dialogue, more reactions from the minor characters, more of a sense of any changes taking place around the action has the effect of speeding up the action, because the story becomes fuller, more complete.

Now let's examine the way in which Ed expanded his experience in the typhoon from a three-page first draft into a ten-page epic struggle.

THE TYPHOON OF FORTY-FIVE
by Edward R. Boyle

FIRST DRAFT

As a young sailor in 1945, I served as a signalman aboard a patrol craft. These ships were not large. Just 125 feet long and 28 feet wide. During wartime they carried a crew of 125 men.

Our station at this time was three miles outside the harbor of Okinawa. We were on picket duty guarding against submarines and enemy aircraft.

At around eleven we received word that there was a storm. We had noticed the ocean swells were getting larger, but no message was recorded in the log. The captain radioed the watch and also doubled the lookouts for clouds and for any change that might appear in the ocean.

Most of us were young men and had been through storms at sea before, so we gave it little thought. Little did we know what was in store for us.

My regular watch this day was from 12:00 noon to 4:00 P.M. I arrived on the bridge at 11:45 A.M. The signalman on duty informed me of the orders which had been issued. I relieved him and took charge of the bridge.

All was serene for the first hour of my watch. Then the sea became a little more restless, the swells a little larger and we could see a few white caps. Still no clouds in the sky, however.

The captain, sensing trouble I'm sure, ordered all watertight hatches closed. All of the equipment that might shift was securely tied down. We all got into our foul-weather gear, for we knew that there was going to be some kind of trouble. All hands that were not needed had been sent below. Those who remained on deck were the captain, the boatswain's mate, two lookouts and myself.

It wasn't long after these precautions were taken that the lookout shouted, "Rain clouds to the southwest. Ten to fifteen miles." All eyes immediately turned in that direction. From southeast to northwest and as high as we could see into the sky was the most terrifying sight I have ever seen. It was not only night descending upon us but it was fearful lightning and crashing thunder. Being pushed ahead of this was a howling wind that screeched like a herd of banshees, and rain that felt like a thousand needles that tried to drive right through you.

Within minutes our ship was engulfed in the most awe-inspiring yet terrifying spectacle I believe nature can produce. Our ship was bounced like a cork upon the water. Lightning flashed around us so close that I was sure I could reach out and touch it. Immediately after the flash the thunder was so loud it made the ship shudder. We could hear the *steel* in the ship strain as it was being *twisted* almost beyond its limits.

The initial fear did not last long. There was too much to do. The Captain was giving orders to the wheelhouse as to the course and speed we were trying to maintain. The lookouts had lashed themselves to their posts to keep from being washed overboard. The boatswain's mate and I were working the searchlights because by that time the sea had a lot of floating debris that had broken loose from moorings in the harbor.

We finally received orders to get inside of the harbor where there would be a little more protection. We were able to enter the harbor dodging all manner of floating junk.

Our main purpose now was to find something to tie up to. We finally spotted an anchor buoy. The captain asked Boats, "If I pass close enough can you jump and grab the ring?" Boats answered, without hesitation, "Yes, sir."

The boatswain hung outside the ship's rail. I held the searchlight on the anchor ring, and the two lookouts stood ready with the securing lines.

The captain kept the ship's speed at five knots and just about scraped the anchor buoy. Boats made the nicest four point landing I'd seen in a long time and he had both hands on the ring. The ship had gone about 50 yards beyond the buoy, so we had to back up to get near it again. We were all tense but were ready. As we neared the buoy the lookouts tossed their lines to Boats. After the bow and stern were secured we all heaved a sigh of relief.

The captain ordered all four of us to his cabin. His only words were, "You men did a good job. Do you know you have been on deck for 20 hours?" Handing us each a half-pint of medical brandy, he said, "Drink this and stay in your sack until you wake up, and thanks, fellows."

◊ ◊ ◊

In the first draft, the storm rages around Ed's ship in a few short paragraphs. Ed himself barely figures in the action.

After listening to the comments of the class, Ed rewrote the story, expanding the episode and making clear what he was doing the entire time. (Please see page 203 for the final version).

In the excerpts that follow, I've italicized the words Ed took from the initial draft. The rest of the story is new.

B
>*The initial fear did not last long. There was too much to do and it had to be done now. The captain was giving the wheelhouse instructions as to course and speed.*

"Hey, Boats, where in hell's the flare gun?" bellowed the captain between cracks of thunder.

"It's in the small arms locker, sir."

The captain hesitated just a few moments. "We're going to need that gun on the bridge."

Now I was worried. The flare gun is used only if there is some grave emergency aboard ship, emergencies where the crew is in danger and may need to be rescued. I scrunched down into my foul-weather gear, hoping the captain couldn't see me. The next order I heard was, "Hey, Boyle, get that flare gun."

Now, suddenly, we realize Ed is a significant part of what's going on and that he is headed for some kind of trouble. The dialogue he has added gives us a strong sense of urgency.

Ed then takes us down into the bowels of the ship as he goes in search of the flare gun.

...it was necessary for me to crawl through another horizontal tube to the engine room, a tube ten feet long and three feet high with only room to crawl on all fours. After entering I still had to shut the door behind me. This tube had no lights. Closing it was like sealing my own tomb.

Finally he gets out of the tube and into the crew's quarters where he is at least able to stand.

A
> The noise of the storm was deafening in the crew's quarter. Every time a crash of thunder hit, it sounded like a sledgehammer being driven against the hull.... Inside the ship *the sound of twisting steel* and the popping of rivets was magnified a hundredfold. I had my arms around the mast when an especially loud crash of thunder hit. As the ship rolled to port, I felt the mast twisting in my arms.

None of this wonderful description of action and feelings is in Ed's first draft. This is *expanding the climax*.

When you begin rewriting your story, identify the climax and see if you have given it the attention it needs. If not, then make that central moment richer, deeper, fuller by expanding it.

CONCLUSION

As we have seen, much of our best work emerges from the rewriting of our stories. So look over your stories and see if they can be improved by improvising some dialogue, by defining and then staying close to your story's spine, by finding the best possible beginning to your story, and by expanding its climax beyond a few sentences.

If you will take the time to follow these steps in rewriting, you will be surprised and pleased at how interesting and believable you have made your stories.

CHAPTER SIX

WRITING ABOUT
THE INNER YOU

To know what we are feeling as events are taking place around us is a very special human capability. Psychologists and psychotherapists spend countless hours helping their clients "get in touch" with themselves, meaning, in part, developing the capacity to become aware of their feelings. You may recall that we discussed this awareness in an earlier chapter. By means of the third eye, we said, we may become aware of our feelings. The ability to transfer these feelings onto paper is what makes us writers: With the right words, we can penetrate through to a reader's heart.

COMPOSING

We will now discuss in more detail two kinds of narratives which reveal these feelings. One type describes events and activities in the outside world, which can be seen by many people. The second type is the journey through the inner world of our thoughts and feelings, which can be seen by others only if we bring it to them with the storyteller's art.

Emotion surrounding objects

The following is an example of the first type of narrative, which takes place in the outside world.

HOUSES

by Eugene Mallory

The year is 1935. It is a bad year in Iowa. In 1933 the farm industry had no prices. Most commodities were not worth enough to pay the freight to market. Livestock, not worth the little it cost to feed them, roamed the country roads. In 1934 the drought came and very little grew. Prices went up but there was little to sell. Now in 1935 crops are fair but prices are falling like wounded ducks. The whole state, already drained of money, is thinking, "Here we go again."

The place is Lincoln Way, "fraternity row," Ames, Iowa. I have just stopped the car in a spray of flying sand at the curb. Something is wrong. The Chi Phi house, the house that was never dark, is now dark and stares blankly back at me.

Dorothy, my wife of two years, is with me. We are on our way to the house in Hampton were I grew up. We both know at once what must have happened, but neither wishes to say.

The Chi Phi house had been home to me during the years after my mother's death. My father had lain upstairs in the Hampton house, lost in the ruined corridors of his mind. What horrors he found there he could not, or would not say. One look into his eyes made the looker grateful for the silence. I had fled that house as soon as I could, and found refuge here, a second home. Now it, too, is gone.

The Chi Phi alumni had owned this house. A downtown bank had owned the mortgage. The bank had ended in that strange, sad holiday, the bank holiday of 1933. As long as the student residents could generate enough revenue for the alumni to keep up interest and taxes, the house went on. The alumni had made up shortages before, but were too hard-pressed themselves to do so again. The bank liquidators had no choice either. The word was "foreclose." How many dreams and plans and lives, too, had been foreclosed in those bitter years! The word hovers, a chilling presence in the air between us, but we do not speak. I think I can make out the Chi Phi name plate beside the door and say, "I think I can see the name still there. I am going to look." I leave, before a woman's realism can end the faint and futile hope.

Halfway up the wall I am sure the bronze is there. CHI PHI. We did not flash our Greek around. The Greek was reserved for the plain red and gold badge. "Badge, not pin, you clod." I touch the name plate to be sure. The door is locked. It should not be, but unless repaired, the back door cannot be locked.

I go across the lawn and down the steep rutted drive. The flat unpaved lot holds no cars, or does it? There is something at the back. I have a little feeble light. A flash and I recognize the hulk. Stu's ancient and decrepit Auburn Speedster. It had brought him from Chicago in style, but once down the drive it never had the strength to bring itself back up. I turn away, leaving the carcass in its trap.

I head for the kitchen door, pushing aside almost tangible memories. Freddy Wilson's new hat, the endless verses of "God, but it's cold in Iowa." The door yields as I knew it would. The outside air is sharp with cold. Inside, the air is colder still, and lifeless and heavy in the chest. What was in this house? I had met death in that other house, on the days when caskets banked in flowers had stood before the curved glass of the parlor windows and old Mr. Beebe came to leave his card and pay his respects to those whose lives had worn away. That was a house where death had come. What went with death, death and desolation? Desolation has come here.

A verse from scripture I had learned in this house comes slowly back to mind. The Chi Phi founding fathers had used it in the ritual they wrote a hundred years ago. It was natural, since six of the twelve had Reverend before their names: " ... the flower of the field flourisheth. The wind passeth over it. The place thereof knows it no more." Indeed, some ancient seed has passed and here it will be no more.

I suddenly realize that, lost in thought, I am wasting my feeble light. Do I need a light to think? I snap it off and soon find that in this place, in this darkness, I do not think so well. The light comes back a little stronger, and I decide to look into the dining room.

Something is crunching underfoot, the Chi Phi china smashed upon the floor. Vandals have been here, the tribe that ravaged Rome. Could they never die?

The huge oval table is still there but my light will hardly reach its length. It has been stripped and only rags of padding cover the naked lumber.

I call back the vision of the last formal dinner I saw here. The small town and country boys sweating in their stiff collars, hard shirt fronts and black bow ties. Our dandy, Meliher, at ease and resplendent in white tie and tails. The girls, bare arms and shoulders gleaming in the candle light. The strapless ones a bit uneasy as to just how much was gleaming.

All so young, rehearsing the glamour and sophistication of the lives they hoped to lead. The vision is hard to hold. The malignant gloom devours the candlelight. My little light is fading too, its battery sucked dry by the darkness and the cold. It is time to go.

When I reach the car, I tell the news, "I got in all right, but they are gone, and the place was vandalized."

Dorothy puts her arms about me and says, "You're shivering Gene. Let's go home."

That car is new and fast. No killing wind can pass over us this night. The Hampton house is home again.

The next time I was on fraternity row, the Chi Phi house was gone and the basement yawned, an open grave. The details of the break-up, I never knew. No one was ever hopeful enough even to write and ask for money.

Money and hope were both in short supply in the Iowa of 1935.

◊ ◊ ◊

You will notice that each object described in this story has an enormous past. When such an object is described effectively, it can have a strong emotional impact on the reader or listener. This concept is similar in many ways to one of the exercises used by actors trained in the Stanislavski system, called "circumstances surrounding an object." In this exercise, the actor builds a past life around an object so that, when it is used on stage or on film, the audience will see and feel the connections to the past—the happy, sad, poignant memories connected with the object.

To give an example from my own life, the interior of the car I own, a 1964 Volvo, has a wonderful smell to it. It is a distinctive smell, one which everyone who climbs into the car notices. But only I know that it is a smell almost identical to my father's Packard, a car I loved, a smell which reminds me of a happy time in my life when I was small and my father was alive and showing me things in and around Detroit, things which I saw and experienced for the first time.

Expressing inner emotion

The second type of narrative is that in which an event in the outside world triggers a flood of inner feelings, often conflicting ones. As with non-objective paintings such as those of Wassily Kandinsky or Jackson Pollock, the emotions may become detached from the object which inspired them. Or there may continue to be some reference to the object. In the late paintings of artists such as J.M.W. Turner (*The Fighting Téméraire, The Morning After the Deluge*) and Claude Monet (*Water Lilies*), there is always a hint of the object in the abstract swirls of emotion on the canvas.

Occasionally, the emotions of the inner world rise to the surface and appear as part of the outer world in a surprising and revealing portrait of the writer's own emotional landscape. As an example of this, please read Rose Rothenberg's story, "Young Love" (see page 94).

These stories are fine examples of a strong awareness of emotions being part of the subject of the narrative. In "Houses" the objects are so filled with emotion that we, the readers, feel that emotion as well. In "Young Love" the writer's emotions are the subject of the story, and we feel her pain as she struggles to return to normal feelings, a struggle we have all experienced at one time or another.

Here, then, are the four steps to follow when writing from within.

1. Follow all the steps we have already discussed to set clearly in your mind a story or incident which you would like to narrate.

2. Review the story or incident which is in your mind, recollecting how you felt with each turn of events during the story.

3. Recall not only your emotions and those of any other central character, but also how other, specific people around you responded to the situation.

4. Allow yourself to make your own emotions— your sadness, pain, awe, amusement, fascination, etc.—the subject of certain episodes.

◊ ◊ ◊

The following are some inner emotions that deserve attention:

— Aloneness, when my parents left me

— Nakedness, when I did something very embarrassing

— Exhilaration, when I did something unique

— Sadness, when someone dear to me left me, never to return

— Frustration, when something I tried and tried to do continued to be impossible to accomplish

— Peace, when some lengthy struggle finally came to a satisfying conclusion

— Yearning, when something I wanted very much became even more desirable than before

— Awe, when something I participated in took on a life of its own

— Anger, when forces beyond my control shaped the lives of those around me

◊ ◊ ◊

Now it is time for me to explore some events which hold some of my deepest feelings and emotions . . . I am traveling back over my sea of memories . . . I am beginning to see the moment . . . it is time to write . . . **now.**

◊ ◊ ◊

REVIEWING

In reviewing your story at this point, you may ask yourself: Is it unfolding naturally and easily, and are the emotional responses of the central character, the writer, and others also quite clear?

And to our checklist on the following page we now add one final item: the presence of the writer's own emotions as the subject of his or her life's stories.

CONCLUSION

You now have the techniques you need to write your life stories, to express your inner feelings as well as describe people and events in the outside world. In your subsequent stories, try to achieve an effective balance of narration, dialogue, and inner monologue. Not every story requires such a balance, but most stories will be enhanced by it. And remember to use your inner thoughts and feelings, to write from within.

LIFE WRITING CHECKLIST

1. Is my story visual?

2. Are my feelings in the story?

3. Is the story told from a consistently believable point of view—a child's, perhaps? Am I using the first person and the present tense?

4. Do the details make the story clearer and more interesting?

5. Does the dialogue help tell the story and make the characters more interesting? Does the dialogue convey a sense of the relationships among the characters?

6. Have I kept to one well-focused incident at a time (or several well-focused incidents if I am writing about an interesting character)?

7. Are the characters' qualities evident?

8. Have I set the stage properly and given some background if necessary?

9. Have I looked into my innermost feelings for the truth of the story?

10. Have I improvised toward the facts where my memory needs some help? Particularly in adding dialogue?

11. Do I have a spine to the story? Have I begun the story in the right place? Is the climax expanded enough?

12. Are my own emotions the subject of any part of the story?

CHAPTER SEVEN

DEVELOPING
SUPPORTIVE FEEDBACK

AT THIS POINT, I WANT TO STEP BACK FROM OUR work on technique to talk about the process of giving and getting criticism. A key aspect of succeeding as a writer is knowing when and where to get guidance, support, and assistance. As writers, most of us need feedback from members of a writers' group, an editor, or some other trusted source. I want to suggest ways of getting positive support and feedback and to tell you how to get the most out of it in order to continue to grow in your work.

We have all encountered criticism from different people during our lives. We probably remember how stung we felt when teachers, parents, and even friends criticized us when we were doing the best we could. Such criticism felt particularly harsh when we were doing something artistic—writing, painting, drawing, or playing a musical instrument. Often, we simply stopped doing these artistic things. Gradually, we internalized this criticism and developed our own inner critic.

Now that we are going to do some writing, we need

to retrain this inner critic. Otherwise, we may not go on writing after the first bit of harsh criticism we receive when we share our work with others—and we *do need* feedback.

Retraining one's inner critic is no small or easy task. It can be accomplished, however, by patience, discipline, and a positive outlook. The same process can also be used to retrain the critic within members of your support structure. First, let us consider the kind of feedback we as writers would *like* to experience. Then I will outline a process by which the wild, undisciplined, even destructive critic within yourself can be converted to a purposeful, disciplined, insightful one.

WHAT IS SUPPORTIVE FEEDBACK?

A group, or even one like-minded person, can help you get the kind of feedback you need. This person or group to whom you are going to turn for support needs to develop a disciplined response to your writing, to protect you and make you feel safe while guiding you in the direction of better work.

That discipline involves adhering strictly to the following agreement which each participant will make with other participants: Feedback to each writer after he or she shares a story will be Non-Judgmental, Non-Invasive, Corrective, and Affirming (NJNICA, for short). Each person giving feedback agrees to avoid any statement that sounds judgmental or invasive, no matter how innocently he or she intends it. During the early sessions of any group one person may be appointed to be on the lookout for such judgmental and invasive statements.

A. Typical judgmental statements are:

> You *should* have.... You *could* have.... You *ought* to have ....
> If *I* were you, *I* would ....

> That (story, thought, paragraph, etc.) was *too* (sentimental, clever, abrupt, silly, slow, confusing, boring, etc.)

B. Typical invasive questions and statements are:

> Why did (or didn't) you ... ?
> Why were you ... ?
> You sound like you were trying ....
> You often ... or always ....

Any one of these statements can discourage a writer. Instead, ask members of your group to try

A. Non-judgmental corrective statements such as:

> I would like to (see, feel, know, be able to follow, etc.) ....
> I had trouble seeing the picture.
> I had difficulty following the action.
> I needed to feel the character's feelings.
> I found my attention wandering.
> I needed to hear the characters talk to each other more.
> I had difficulty finding (or following) the spine.
> I didn't know what the central question of the story was.
> The key question was answered before I had a chance to get involved or get excited about it.

B. Non-judgmental affirming statements such as:

> I saw the picture clearly.
> I was right there with you the whole time.
> I knew what each character (or the narrator) was feeling from one moment to the next.
> The dialogue drew me in and helped me know each character.
> The balance of narrative, dialogue, and inner thoughts and feelings held my interest.

These are important considerations. A potential writer can listen all day to by non-judgmental, non-invasive, corrective, and affirming (NJNICA) comments. He can listen for only a few moments to invasive or judgmental statements. Then he will begin to defend himself, his creativity will turn off, and he will stop writing.

You may find that your support system is only one person, or perhaps you and a friend decide to write your life stories and share them. One person is enough if his or her feedback is non-invasive, non-judgmental, corrective, and affirming.

The great advantage of working in a group or with a friend is that the writer can stop being the critic and simply create. Each person can then be a responsible critic for the other writers when they read their stories. So keep looking for one or two people with whom you can share this special journey of self-exploration.

However, if the person you select to review your work simply says, "I like it," or "I don't like it," and shows no inclination to go beyond this, get a new partner. Likewise, if he or she makes judgmental or invasive comments, find someone who *is* willing to provide NJNICA feedback. If you find yourself alone and unable to develop a writer-reviewer relationship with any-one, then try to develop these NJNICA qualities in yourself.

If you are a teacher and you wish to encourage your students to write their life stories, it is important to develop habits of NJNICA feedback in them.

The exercises below will help you develop NJNICA feedback, and may be tried alone or in a group.

1. Review each of the following stories

    A. "Willem" (1) (p. 22)
    B. "Goose Story" (1) (p. 64)
    C. "The Typhoon of Forty-Five" — First Draft (p. 68)

2. Give yourself and your friend or group at least one session per story, perhaps one or two sessions a week.

   Appoint one person to roleplay the "writer" of each story. If you are that writer, you may *defend* what has been written any time you feel the feedback is hostile, judgmental, invasive, or superficial. When the critique of "your" work is over, tell the others what it felt like: who was providing NJNICA feedback and who was not.

3. If you are giving feedback, describe your responses to the story aloud. If you are doing this alone, talk into a tape recorder, or speak aloud, or, as a last resort, write it down.

   Focus your attention on how you responded to the story rather than on how the story is written (i.e., "I needed more detail," "I found my attention wandering," etc., rather than "It's too long, too confusing," etc.).

   If the person roleplaying the writer begins to defend himself, it is a clue that you or others in the group are being judgmental or invasive or superficial. Find a NJNICA comment that will make the point.

   Remember, by giving NJNICA feedback which focuses on your reactions to the story, you leave the writer room to make choices about what to change and what not to change.

   Have each person in the group defend or absorb feedback for five minutes. Continue until each person in the group has had a chance to roleplay the writer. The comments may be repetitive, but the purpose of the task is to experience (1) being a writer under the gun, and (2) changing your mode of giving feedback from judgmental or superficial to NJNICA.

4. Address the following issues:

   A. "Willem" (1)

   — Is the point of view child or adult?
   — Is the story written in the present or as a recollection?
   — Is the level of language child or adult?
   — Is the situation believable?
   — Are the writer's feelings clearly expressed?

   B. "Goose Story" (1)

   — Is the picture clear?
   — Are the writer's feelings clearly expressed?
   — Where should the dialogue begin?
   — Where should the "setting the stage" material go?

   C. "The Typhoon of Forty-Five"—First Draft

   — Is the picture clear?
   — Are the writer's feelings clearly expressed?
   — Do we need more details? What kind?
   — Do we need more dialogue? What kind?
   — Do we get the feelings of the narrator moment to moment?
   — Is the story's meaning clearly expressed?

5. When the initial critique of each story is complete, read the final version of the story aloud, again appointing a writer to defend or explain the work. Remember, there are no *right* answers to the issues. We are attending to the task of creating feedback and promoting lively discussions.

6. After the third session, you will be ready for feedback on your own stories. If you have not written your earliest memories yet, read the first two chapters in the book, then follow the

steps below if you have one or more persons giving feedback.

A. Tell your earliest memory aloud into a tape recorder or to your friend or group. Get a few NJNICA comments, then retell the story in the present tense: "I am five years old and I am ..." rather than "I was ...."

B. Write your story just as you have told it aloud. If the group is large or time is running short, do the writing at home, but try to do the writing immediately.

C. Repeat NJNICA feedback for each story.

D. Each writer in the group should repeat the storytelling/writing process until they are comfortable writing and receiving feedback. At this point, the writing can be done at home.

Remember that each new person added to the group or class needs to be taken through this storytelling/writing process. New group members need to be encouraged to listen for NJNICA feedback, and given a little time to develop NJNICA feedback. With practice and time, the whole group's feedback—and unity—will be all the better for it!

In Part II we will move on to writing about a wide range of experiences. These stories will come naturally, if not easily, when you have completed the stories and exercises in Part I.

As a conclusion to Part I, let me emphasize again the importance of writing your earliest memory and of writing from a child's point of view. These are the exercises that will develop your roots as a writer and allow you to find your authentic voice.

PART TWO

WRITING
THE SIGNIFICANT MOMENTS
IN YOUR LIFE

CHAPTER EIGHT

LIFE STAGES
AND THE JOURNEY

YOU NOW HAVE A WEALTH OF WRITING TECHNIQUES AT your fingertips and, after several weeks, perhaps months, of working on your memoirs, have probably recorded quite a few memories from your childhood.

In fact, you probably have as much technique as you will ever need. Oh, your style will improve as you learn to edit your work more carefully, and your dialogue will become sharper as you listen closely to the conversations of those around you (try not to be too obvious when you are listening!). But, all in all, you have the basic techniques you need.

You are now ready to take on more complicated experiences. The memories of childhood are so powerful that they form wonderful stories almost by themselves. Adult life, on the other hand, is rather like a vast sea. A few things really stand out, but, mostly, our life is a series of larger and smaller ripples that spread out around us as we move in different directions.

The decision to write one's life's stories is a decision to embark on a voyage of recollection and rediscovery, to find the things that really moved and affected us, and shaped our lives. As we tack back and forth across the sea of life, we will see a number of markers or buoys floating at anchor on either side of our channel of memories. Just as buoys signal to ships where the deep water passages lie, so our memory buoys will mark the important events of our lives, guiding us away from the reefs of trivial or unimportant experience and moving us toward our destination: the understanding of our lives and the shaping of our passage through time into memorable, timeless stories.

Some of these markers signal truly significant stages of our lives: romance, work, war, marriage, career, children, retirement, grandchildren, second careers, and the death of loved ones. These act as powerful signals for our writing, not only as places to begin our narratives but also as markers on which to set our sights. Some lives are especially tumultuous, filled with waves, and these markers help such people discover their own proper channel through the sea of memories.

For most of us, revisiting these memories will be painful as well as joyous, consuming as well as satisfying. But remember that revisiting a painful past may be one of the most therapeutic things we can do for ourselves. By putting the experience on paper, reading it aloud, and hearing our words, we can begin to let go of it. Or perhaps we could say that it will let go of us.

At the same time, the incidents may show themselves to be part of a larger narrative, and they will take on a different meaning for us. We will begin to see patterns in our lives.

Perhaps, in all honesty, we view our lives as failures. We may find that an accurate retelling of the first episode of this "failure" could lead to a reconciliation with relatives and friends whom we long ago alienated in some way. Or perhaps we were headed in a dull, ordinary, or pedestrian direction when one of these "firsts" occurred, redirecting our lives, and now we understand the meaning and value of the experience.

Virtually every religion on this earth has, at its center, a person who has undergone a journey of some kind, who has been through a number of trials and emerged on the other side in some way transformed or reborn. That heroic journey, so well chronicled by mythologist Joseph Campbell, is not the sole province of great or important men and women. In one way or another we are all embarked on our life's journey, are tested by life, and have the opportunity to be reborn. Some of us will experience this rebirth in the process of writing our life's stories, because only then will our lives make sense.

Two important areas of experience we will need to review are our relationships with our parents and with our children. Often, these relationships have not been entirely happy or, particularly in the case of our children, we may feel the process is not complete. Nevertheless, we need to address these experiences as directly as possible. We have related many experiences from childhood in earlier stories; now, it is time to speak to our parents directly. Experience has shown that once we say what we need to say to our parents, we can then say what we need to say to our children. This is not easy to do, but the rewards are immense.

All of this is preparation for the ultimate experience we face: death. Most of us are fearful about death. We envision a state where our faculties have diminished with age, our loved ones may be gone, and we are alone. But that is only one way of viewing death. There are other ways, and we will discuss them in a later chapter.

When you feel you are ready, look out toward that magnificent sea, step down into the boat of memory and journey to the first buoy in sight: first love.

CHAPTER NINE

FIRST LOVE

AT FIRST GLANCE, ONE MIGHT THINK THAT DESCRIB-
ing a first love is no particular problem. "She/he
was very beautiful/handsome and nice and I just fell in
love." Unfortunately, such a description has a problem—it doesn't really let the reader in on what the
lover thought and felt. How do we go about letting the
reader in on this experience?

There are two qualities which are worth noting in
most stories of first love. First, something has changed
in the life of the narrator, something that allows love to
enter, that makes the narrator vulnerable to love's
arrow. This quality appears and reappears in many
stories of first love, and may also appear in yours. If so,
be aware of this new twist to your life.

The second quality is related to our earlier discussions about the "third eye." We find ourselves recording
what is going on inside us as well as recording what is
happening in the outside world. The ingredients of this
awareness are, in no particular order, a description of
the first person we loved, a description of the incident
or incidents in which the two of us participated, and a

description of how we felt while participating in the experience(s). What makes most stories of first love unusual is the sense that, although there is an objective world out there, when love enters—or leaves—the scene, everything, including the self and perhaps the world, is transformed by a new chemistry, a heightened awareness, as though one has taken a drug of some kind.

In the story that follows, the writer captures some of the extremes of feeling—both high and low—which accompany the experience of first love.

YOUNG LOVE

by Rose Rothenberg

The spring day dawned sunny and bright. The blue of the sky stretched endlessly without cloud interruption. But the day's brilliance could not penetrate my blanket of grayness. I hugged it close to me as I had for days since emerging from the black hole of nothingness to contemplate the bleakness of the new world I had entered.

The shell of my being functioned still in the old world. In the aliveness of this world my shell lived, slept, ate, interacted with family and friends. My true self secreted itself in darkness, wrapped itself in solitary unfeeling grayness. It resisted all efforts to puncture the layers of cloud matter that swirled around me and protected me from hurt.

I alone knew where I was and why—or so I thought. One evening as my shell walked silently beside my brother, he thought to reach me in the colorless beyond where I had escaped, to pull me out into the sunshine with him. "There's more than one fish in the sea," he said.

My shell responded in the flippant way of that other world. "I never did like fish anyway. They can all stay in the sea so far as I'm concerned. Try your

psychology on someone else." And I marched angrily ahead.

My brother, three and a half years my senior,
confident at twenty-two in his role of big brother
and protector, shrugged his shoulders and snorted,
"Forget it—it's not worth being in the dumps about
anyway."

My shell and he continued on our way but my
suffering soul retreated further into the comforting
void.

There came a time when my true self lifted the
protective curtain that enveloped me and peered
into the world I had left. The glare and brightness
of that place was too intense to be faced, and quickly I dropped the gray curtain once more—until the
next time.

As time passed I lifted the curtain more boldly
and was able to absorb the otherworldly brightness
for longer periods. Inevitably there came a day when
I flung the heavy grayness aside completely and
met and merged with my shell. Together and in-
separably we walked once more in the warm sunshine.

I knew then for certain that my first love, my
deep youthful love, my rejected love, would not be
my last love.

◊ ◊ ◊

This story is a glimpse into the writer's inner emotions, first experienced as though her pain is very close
to us. We also see the outer world, represented by her
brother, quite far away as if glimpsed through a tunnel.
By the end of the story she has come to the end of the
tunnel; her emotions have softened. She has returned
to the land of the living.

First love often places demands not only on the
person in love but on everyone else around. When writ-

ing your own story of first love, see if you can recollect
what effect the turmoil in your life and heart had on
those around you. Since most of us are not going to
experience first love again, we can only hope that those
who come after us will have a grandmother as understanding as the one in this next story.

ADVICE TO A FOOLISH VIRGIN
by Bess Shapiro

I'm deeply in love with Bill. I'm also deeply in
lust with Bill. I have just reached my twentieth
birthday. My heart is ready, and my body is clamor-
ing for that mysterious consummation that will
bind us together forever.

But where can that magic take place?

I share a bedroom with Grandma. I complain to
her, after assuring her that she's the dearest room-
mate a girl could have.

"Dammit, Grandma! I don't have any privacy.
What if I want to make a baby with Bill?"

Grandma gives me a sly smile. "Foolish little
girl! Just say to me, 'Grandma, take a walk!' How
long does it take to make a baby? Five minutes."

◊ ◊ ◊

For another delightful experience of first love (or,
perhaps, hormonal love), please turn to "Fessex, Fessex,
Prenez Garde!" by Isidore Ziferstein (page 186).

◊ ◊ ◊

*Perhaps you too feel it is time for you to return to
your place of memory. Find your comfortable spot, close
your eyes, recollect your earliest love, and write . . .*

CHAPTER TEN

YOUNG ADULTHOOD: ADVENTURE AND RESPONSIBILITY

As WE LOOK OUT OVER THE VAST SEA OF OUR LIFE'S experiences, past the marker buoys of childhood memories and first love, we can see one coming up called, perhaps, "first freedom" or "memories of young adulthood."

It is a time when the dependent years of childhood have ended. The first significant phase of education is complete. For some, it means a high school diploma; for others who have worked from an early age, it means some skills have been acquired. It is the first time in our lives we are able to say, "I want to do such-and-such," and can expect to be free to pursue our goals and desires despite any lingering strictures of societal convention, self-expectation, or parental authority.

For some people it is a time of frustration, of decisions made unconsciously and later regretted: a college chosen hastily, a marriage and a family formed unwisely.

This stage of life is also a time when we take on

new responsibilities, a time when work begins to have real significance for us. Education and training may be behind us; enterprise, dedication, and accomplishment are before us. It is also a time when we may take on these responsibilities with some sense of awe at what we have chosen to do. The following is one young man's story of confronting his newly won responsibilities and the expectations of others.

"YOU'RE THE DOCTOR, DOCTOR!"
by Isidore Ziferstein

It's the morning of July 1, 1935, and I'm twenty-five years old, about to begin a two-and-a-half-year stint as an intern at the Jewish Hospital of Brooklyn. All the new interns look a bit young in their crisp, white uniforms, but they exude an air of professionalism and confidence. I know that I look even younger than the rest of the lot, and I feel anything but confident or professional.

I'm aware that from this day on, the lives and the well-being of real human beings may depend on my judgment and on my calm in an emergency. No longer is it simply a matter of getting a good grade or a poor grade when I make a diagnosis, as it had been during my four years in medical school.

The first day passes uneventfully, because the senior intern, George Ruby, bless him, is always at my side, whispering helpful hints as I examine new admissions and, later, make evening rounds.

During the night, I am awakened for a couple of emergencies on the medical wards, but the ever-helpful Dr. Ruby is there by my side. I find myself wishing that he would be by my side for the next two-and-a-half years. Better yet, for the rest of my professional life.

At the second evening's rounds, Ruby is standing back, letting me write the orders. Motherly looking Nurse Greenberg is most helpful.

After the completion of evening rounds, Ruby says, "Ziferstein, you've done very well, for a beginner. And now I can take the night off with a clear conscience. It's all yours! So long!"

I have trouble falling asleep that second night. Half the night, I lie on my narrow cot, eyes wide open, expecting to be jarred at any moment by the loud ringing of the telephone. But all is well until about 3:00 A.M., when I'm awakened out of a fitful sleep by the insistent ringing of the telephone, which sounds more like the crash of thunder.

"Doctor! Emergency on 4 west."

I am not used to being called Doctor. It takes a few seconds for the cobwebs to clear, and for me to realize that this emergency is *my* emergency!

I jump into my trousers, white jacket, and slippers and run to the elevator, my stethoscope trailing behind me as I run.

On 4 West, I see a very obese, middle-aged woman propped up in bed, wheezing loudly, and looking as though she's about to breathe her last. I glance at Nurse Greenberg, who had been so helpful at evening rounds, and I scream, "This looks bad, Nurse! Quick, get a doctor!"

Nurse Greenberg whispers in my ear, "You're the doctor, Doctor!"

Mercifully, she also whispers in my ear what orders I'm supposed to give her. Obediently, in a voice that's a bit too loud and commanding but with a slight tremolo, I give her the orders.

With God's help, and a big assist from the highly experienced Nurse Greenberg, both patient and doctor survive the night.

◊ ◊ ◊

The first half of the story is all narrative but is effective, probably because it is in the present tense. The dialogue is sparse, but each line tells us a lot about the speakers: breezy, jovial Dr. Ruby; panicky, disoriented Isidore; worldly, experienced Nurse Greenberg.

As I read the story, my delight is in its innocence. The narrator is in no way reluctant to let us see him as naïve and inexperienced, as he approaches his initiation. We know that gradually he will grow into the authoritative voice that is a bit too loud and a bit too commanding in the story.

In our memoirs we must honestly acknowledge how we felt about ourselves then and how we feel about those decisions today. In every case, there were probably other choices we could have made, although at first we couldn't see them. So as you sit down to write your memoirs of this very significant period of early freedom, recapture for yourself that mental and physical energy you had, as well as the feelings and emotions which surrounded the choices you made.

This period of young adulthood is also a time of high adventure. The experiences into which we enter, willingly or not, may yield hysterically funny stories. Or they may turn into heroic journeys. It is the time of what Joseph Campbell, author of *The Hero With a Thousand Faces*, terms the " . . . call to adventure," such as the story we discussed earlier, Ed Boyle's "Typhoon of Forty-Five."

◊ ◊ ◊

Now it is your turn. Roll back the pages of the past to the time when you stood on the brink of young adulthood about to be thrust out into a wider world than you had known before. Sit back in that easy chair, perhaps thumb through some old photo albums or newspapers from the time when you were in your late teens. When you are ready, close your eyes, recollect your past, and write.

CHAPTER ELEVEN

"RIGHT YOU ARE IF YOU THINK YOU ARE"

DIFFERING POINTS OF VIEW

FEW EVENTS ARE EVER EXPERIENCED OR REMEMbered the same way by any two people. Most of us argue incessantly that "our" version is more accurate than "their" version is. Some of us, in writing our life's stories, actually modify our own remembrances by including facts and memories of others with whom we shared the experience. "There must be one version of what has happened that is correct," we suppose. Someone has to be right and someone has to be wrong.

One of the more interesting challenges of the 20th century has been to come to grips with the idea that there is no one universal, immutable truth that exists outside our own perceptions. There are only points of view about what exists. If many of those points of view agree, we conclude that those agreeing points of view constitute a truth, at least for the time being. If, however, other, differing points of view arise later on, we do not have to make them wrong or false or unreal. There are only differing truths, particularly where it concerns our memories.

In drama, this was articulated most forcefully in the early years of the 20th century by Luigi Pirandello. His plays *Six Characters in Search of an Author, Tonight We Improvise,* and *Right You Are If You Think You Are* provide us with unusual points of view, each argued powerfully, leaving the playgoers to decide whose version is correct.

If we also approach the writing of our life's stories from the position that there are no "truths," only versions of the truth, then we can respect, admire, even enjoy someone else's version of events or experiences which seem very different to us.

For this exercise, find an event or experience which left a strong impression on you, one which you are certain a close relative or friend of yours viewed quite differently. Correspond with your relative or friend, get some agreement about the event you are recollecting, then each of you write about it. Exchange versions, compare them, then write a commentary about the similarities and differences. My guess is that this task will result in a lot of laughs, or it may lead to a great deal more understanding between you.

The stories below describe a birthday party experienced very differently by two sisters, aged eight and thirteen.

Memories of a
Thirteenth Birthday Party
by Carol Cunningham

My sister Barbara is really a teenager today. Thirteen. She got to have her party last Saturday night. It lasted until eleven o'clock. All the girls got to wear long dresses and the boys had to wear ties. Mom let me go to the party, but I didn't get to wear a long dress. I wish I could have. In a long dress I would have looked older and maybe they wouldn't have treated me like they did.

Everything was so beautiful. Mom had the dining room table all set with flowers and candles and place cards. The place cards were fun. Mom wrote a poem on the place card about everyone who came and then they had to read the poems and figure out which one was about them. Barbara's best friend, Edith, was the easiest. She looks like Betty Grable and the poem said so. Everyone knew where Edith was supposed to sit.

◊ ◊ ◊

MEMORIES OF A THIRTEENTH BIRTHDAY PARTY
by Barbara Lewis

My sister has asked me to tell you about my thirteenth birthday party. Let's see—it's not easy, as I've managed to block out most of my childhood memories in which "she" was involved, the reason being when I was five years old (and up until that time, the only child, the center of my parents' universe) "she" was brought home. I was a blonde, curly-headed charmer and "she" looked like an abandoned Indian papoose who did nothing but lie there and cry. For years I tried unsuccessfully to get rid of her and as "she" grew, "she" became more impossible. My parents assured me that "she" was my real sister, but she was unbelievably skinny, had long, dark, stringy hair that never looked combed, and she collected ghastly paper flowers, also junk of all sorts which "she" managed to wear somewhere on her person. I was sure that everyone thought we had adopted a gypsy waif.

Anyway, "she" was forced on me relentlessly, so at my thirteenth birthday party there was no escape. "She" was to be included and no amount of crying and threatening would budge my parents. The party was a sit-down dinner and dance. All day my mother (who was a marvelous cook) and the maid cleaned and prepared wonderful dishes, the aromas promising great things to eat. At long last it was time for guests to arrive. Guess who was the first to answer the doorbell? "She," of course, greeting my friends, looking for all the world as though the caravan had forgotten her. I could hardly get a word in. Finally everyone arrived. Jean, whose mother was a best-selling author; Edith, whose father owned a chocolate factory; Elenita, my closest friend, who lived across the street in a large mansion surrounded by high walls; Jerry, whom I don't remember very well; Robert, a tall, good-looking German who went to the American School; and Jim, the blond, handsome athlete. We all attended the American School in Monterrey, Mexico. I had been trying to decide whether Robert or Jim was going to be my boyfriend. Whoever responded the most favorably at the party would be the one.

My mother had written poems about each guest; there was one at each place setting and they were to guess which poem identified which guest. My friends were delighted with the descriptions Mother had given them. Dinner over, it was time to dance. My parents went next door. I quickly turned off several lights so there would be a more romantic atmosphere. We picked out records to be played and started dancing. "She" was right there in the middle of the group, embarrassing me, dancing by herself. I had had great plans for dancing cheek to cheek, maybe a kiss or two, but there "she" was, dancing as though "she" were thirteen and be-

longed. I had to do something . . . An inspiration!!!
Lock her in the closet; so we did. What a chore it
was getting her in there, with all the kicking and
screaming. I don't think "she" was in there too
long, but we were able to dance cheek to cheek and
there was some kissing. I also decided Jim was to
be my boyfriend. The details are fuzzy as to what
happened after "she" was let out. All in all, my
party was a success.

"She" is still thin, "she" is still a bit of a gypsy,
and her hair would be straight without a per-
manent. However, "she" is creative, warm, and totally endearing. My closest friend—my sister.

◊ ◊ ◊

The touching little fragment from Carol tells us far
more about what happened than its modest length
would indicate. For Barbara, Carol's presence was an
intrusion on a carefully orchestrated event. Barbara
improvised, got Carol out of the way and got her guy. To
Carol, the party was a wonderful opportunity to be
among older people. We feel her hurt at how things
went awry. We experience her bewilderment at not
knowing what was really going on: "In a long dress I
would have looked older and maybe they wouldn't have
treated me like they did." It is the wonderful, innocent
hurt of the child.

Carol's sketch is also a reminder to us all to get our
versions of the truth out and known, for we may not always have the opportunity to write them. During the
period she was working on this story, Carol suffered a
fatal stroke. The unfinished story lay at her bedside.

In reflecting about the episode you wish to record,
you may conclude that one of the stories you've already
written would do just fine. If that is the case, then by
all means get in touch with the person who may have
experienced this episode differently.

If you wish to begin a new story, remember that one of your objectives is to renew or revive an old relationship, so it is best to tread lightly if the subject is at all controversial or painful. But do not be reluctant to share your feelings as you remember them.

◊ ◊ ◊

Let some vivid memories of incidents or experiences you've shared with others come to mind. Give the people involved a call; ask them to write out heir version. Don't be daunted if someone says no. Find the person who will say yes.

CHAPTER TWELVE

TRAUMA

SCANNING THE HORIZON, WE GLIMPSE SOME MARKER buoys that look quite different from the others. They remain in darkness, as if in perpetual shadows, strange markers, yet vital to our narrative. If we gaze into ourselves, we realize that each marker has a name written on it, a name that is difficult and painful to read, scrawled at an angle so that we can barely see it: TRAUMA.

These markers give us a chilly clue to the experiences which lie beneath. Perhaps we would like to pass them by, but we must not.

These traumas may be genuine tragedies, intensely experienced, maybe even caused by ourselves. Now is the time for us to view them clear-sightedly. Most often, they will be the untimely deaths of people we love. Often, too, they may be shocking injuries to someone we love, or even to ourselves. When writing about these experiences, there are four things we must do.

First, we must prepare for reliving the experience and writing about it; just as an athlete goes into training, we must go into training. And just as a part of training and conditioning is mental—"psyching up" for the task, visualizing good things happening—so we must encourage ourselves by congratulating ourselves, telling ourselves what a good thing it is we are doing.

Second, we must finish the story once we have started it. Despite the tears and pain, we must keep writing.

Third, we need to maintain our objectivity, and not blame anyone. As the writer, our job is to make the reader see the truth, to describe to the reader what we see and experience and feel, so that the reader goes through that pain or feeling or experience.

Fourth, we need to resist the temptation to editorialize or moralize about what has happened. We are storytellers; we need to tell stories. Sometimes, at the end of a tragic or traumatic experience, we do come to certain conclusions about the way the universe operates. If this happens to us, it is appropriate to say something. And it is perfectly alright to express confusion and bewilderment at the nature and power of the Creator of us all. But keep it real. One honest observation is worth more than all the platitudes in the world.

◊ ◊ ◊

These four points will help you through remembering and writing the painful episodes among your life's stories.

Here is such an experience written by one of our writers. You may wish to look closely at it to see if it implements the four suggestions given above, and whether the story is helped by them.

FISHING

by Cathy Smith (pseudonym)

"Fish-ing, fish-ing, I am fish-ing," I sing out loud as I bounce the stick with a string tied onto it for a line and an uncurled paper clip for a hook.

My name is Cathy Smith, and I'm four years old. It's Saturday and I am staying with my mother and her new husband, Terry, for the weekend. I live with my grandmother during the week because Mommy has to go to work. This weekend Mommy went to get her hair done and this is the first time I've ever been alone with my new stepfather.

I haven't decided yet if I like him or not. He is very big, much bigger than my Daddy, and he has no hair on the top of his head. He likes to tickle me when we all sit on the couch together watching television. Sometimes he wrestles with me and throws me up in the air or hangs me upside down by my legs so my skirt falls over my face and I can't see.

I've very busy fishing, trying to stay away from him and wishing Mommy was here, but he keeps watching me and follows me from room to room. I'm in the bedroom now, sitting on the bed with the string hanging off the edge onto the floor. I'm pretending I'm sitting on a rock and dangling my pole into the water. He sits down on the bed next to me and reaches over to tickle me.

"No," I say. "I'm fishing and you're going to spoil it." I move down the bed to get farther away from him.

"Come here," he says.

"No, I want to fish." I get off the bed. "Fish-ing, fish-ing, I am fish-ing," I start singing, so he'll know I'm serious.

He gets up and moves toward me. "Come here," he says again, and picks me up. He takes the fishing pole out of my hand and throws it on the floor. "Lie down with me a minute."

"No," I say, squirming in his arms. "I don't want to." I push against his chest and kick my legs to try to get down. Still holding me, he sits on the bed and swings his legs up so he's lying down with me on top of him.

He's hurting me, and I struggle to get away. "Let me go," I tell him. "I don't want to lie down. I don't have to take a nap yet."

He's breathing hard and his face looks shiny. "Just for a minute," he says, holding me tight across his chest with one arm and reaching between my legs and pulling my panties down with the other one. They get caught on my shoes and won't come all the way off. Then he unzips his pants and I feel something hard press against my stomach.

I don't understand. I don't know what this is, but it feels bad and I'm very frightened. "Let me go," I whimper. "I'm going to tell Mommy when she gets back." I start to cry.

"Shut up," he says, and grabs my hair and pulls my head back so I can see his face. He is pulling hard on my hair and it hurts, but the look on his face makes me forget that. "Shut up and don't move until I'm done. I don't want to hurt you, but I will if you cry." I shut up and lie still. "Open your legs."

"No," I gasp, "it hurts." He yanks my hair again. "Do it," he says. I can only open my legs a little bit because my panties are stuck around my ankles. Then he starts sliding my body up and down so the hard thing rubs against where I go to the bathroom. The zipper is sharp and cuts into my skin every time he moves me. He is breathing through his mouth now and making groaning sounds. Then he makes a big "Ah-h-h" and stops moving my body. The hard thing jerks and it's all wet between my legs. He loosens his grip on me and I just lie there, afraid to move.

He pushes me off him, and I scramble off the bed, trying to get into the bathroom where I can shut the door and get away from him. I can't move right because my panties are still around my ankles, and I trip and fall.

Now he's above me, yanking my arm and pulling me to my feet. "Bad girl," he shouts at me. "You're a very bad girl," he shouts again and slaps me across the face. "If you ever tell anybody what happened, I'll kill you."

"I didn't do anything," I cry back at him. "You did it. I was just fishing, and you hurt me and made me all wet."

"Shut up," he yells, slapping me again. "It was your fault. You're a bad girl. You made me do it. Look at me, Cathy," he says. Still holding my arm, he leans down and puts his face close to mine. "If you ever tell your mother about this, if you ever tell *anybody* about this, I'll kill you." His face is awful. It's all red and his eyes are bulging, and I'm sure he's going to kill me right now. "Do you understand? You won't ever talk about this to anyone— not your mother, not your grandmother, not anybody, ever!" He shakes me really hard and throws me to the floor.

I scream, "I promise. I won't tell. Please don't kill me. I promise I won't tell anybody."

"You better not," he says and yanks me to my feet. "Just remember what will happen to you if you do." I look at him and shake my head, yes. I think he believes me.

He stands there and stares at me for a long time. His face changes color; it's not red anymore. "Oh, god," he says quietly. "Let's get you cleaned up before your mother gets home," and takes me into the bathroom and wipes my legs with a washcloth and pulls up my panties. I don't move. I hardly breathe as he touches me. "Now get out of here and go outside and play until your mother comes home. You've been a bad girl and I can't stand to look at you."

I start to walk toward the front door, and see

the fishing pole lying on the floor. I don't want to play with it anymore. "Cathy," he says, and I stop. "I mean it about not telling."

"I won't," I say, and open the door and go outside.

I sit on the steps and hug my knees to my chest. I sit very, very still and wait for my mother to come back. I don't remember all of what happens after that. She comes back and we have dinner and watch television like we always do. This time, though, I sit on the other end of the couch as far away from him as I can get. When it's time for me to go to bed, Mommy takes me into the bedroom and tucks me in the big bed. I always go to sleep there at first, and then later they move me back to the couch and that's where I wake up in the morning.

The bedroom is dark except for the light coming in through the opened door. The darkness scares me and I start remembering everything again.

"Good night, pumpkin," Mommy says, giving me a hug. "Do you feel all right? You've been so quiet tonight." She feels my forehead with her hand. I start to cry. I don't want her to go. I don't want to be alone in the big bed in the dark. "What's wrong, sweetheart?" she asks, her voice getting soft.

"Mommy, I want to go home. I want to sleep in my bed at Grandma's." I'm choking on my tears and holding on to her as hard as I can. I don't want to be all alone in the big bed where the bad thing happened. "Take me home to Grandma," I plead. "I don't want to stay here any more."

He hears me and comes in and stands in the doorway. "What's the matter with her?" he says. "Why is she crying?"

"I don't know." Her back is to the door and she turns her head and looks over her shoulder at him. "She says she wants to go back to my mother's."

She faces me again and holds me close. "Honey, what's wrong? Why do you want to go back to Grandma's?"

I'm feeling safe with her arms around me and her breath warm on my cheek. "He hurt me," I start to say. My face is buried in her neck and I look through her hair and see him standing in the door. He takes a step forward and raises his arm, his hand closing into giant fist. Silently, he shakes it at me. He looks like some kind of huge monster, his body outlined by the light and filling up the whole door. I can feel waves of something awful coming at me from him.

Mommy starts to turn toward him, and he drops his arm. "I had to spank her while you were gone. She's just making a fuss. Leave her alone," he says. "Cathy, lie down and be quiet or I'll give you something to really cry about. Remember what I told you this afternoon."

I try to stop crying, gulping in air and making snuffling sounds. I was going to tell, and now he's going to kill me. He's going to kill me and Mommy so nobody will ever find out.

"Cathy," Mommy says, "Is that true? Were you a bad girl while I was gone?"

"Yes," I whisper.

"See," he says. "She's just acting up. Come out here and leave her alone."

"Cathy, you know I told you that you have to do what Terry tells you to. He's your Daddy now and he loves you. Go to sleep, honey. I'll leave the door open a little so it won't be so dark."

She kisses me and snuggles me back under the covers. He's waiting at the door and she goes out ahead of him. He turns back to me and holds up his fist again. "Don't you ever try that again," he hisses, and shuts the door all the way.

I start to cry. I can't make the tears stop, but I'm careful to be quiet so he won't hear me and come back in. My face feels hot and places in my body still hurt from him. I curl myself up tight, trying to make the dark and the fear and the shame I feel go away. I was just fishing, but he said it was my fault. He said I'm a bad girl. Mommy must think I'm bad, too, and that's why she didn't leave the door open. Bad girls have to stay alone in the dark and never tell anyone. I won't tell. I won't tell anyone ... ever.

◊ ◊ ◊

We experience quite a range of emotions in this story. Wonder at Cathy's innocent and childlike imagination; confusion, uncertainty, and a strange foreboding about of this new person in her life; fear, pain, and helplessness as she tries to protect herself; sadness, even rage at what is happening to this innocent and delightful child. Cathy's dialogue is vivid, her narrative lean and fast-moving, the point of view very believable as a child's, and the characterizations powerful. The dialogue at the beginning starts a motif that recurs throughout the story, and the terrible central event has been expanded so we feel a full range of emotions.

◊ ◊ ◊

It is very important for us to face up to the traumas of our lives and write about them using all our skill and effort. Getting them out of ourselves and into the open releases us from the burden of carrying around all the guilt and pain that has weighed upon us for so long. The more honestly we write about the event, the more fully we will let go of it.

Some of the very best work done in my classes has come from people who not only put their pain down on paper but put it down eloquently, not as a complaint but as an object for themselves and others to experience and contemplate.

By no means is the pain and anger of the past always going to result in painful, angry stories. Some of the funniest stories come from bottled up anger. A few deft strokes of the pen and a stupid parent becomes an absurd and short-sighted little person.

It also helps sometimes to work against the dominant side of oneself in writing. If we tend to be complainers about life in the present, it may help us to find the good and wonderful things that happened to us in the past. If we tend to be always rosy, it may be wise to look beneath the surface of our lives and confront some of the darker moments. Every life has them. We will find that the more of the one side we confront, the more of the other side will gradually emerge. The more the pain gets cleared away through writing, the more the pleasure of life will reappear, and vice versa. We will find that our memories will begin to return with surprising clarity.

But keep in mind that we don't want to *think* about writing. We want to write. Picking up the pen and simply writing, even if we have nothing specific in mind, is the strongest commitment we can make to getting our life down on paper. Once the pen moves, images will begin to come back. So keep the pen moving. Later we can find out where the actual story should start. When confronting trauma or any difficult episode, the best way to begin is to begin.

◊ ◊ ◊

Now it is time for you to look into the waters beneath that shadowy marker and relive once again some of the things you had hoped would remain hidden from view for the rest of your life. Congratulate yourself for your courage. You deserve it. Go ahead—jump in and start swimming. The results will amaze you. Believe me.

CHAPTER THIRTEEN

THE LOVE(S)
OF YOUR LIFE

As we continue across the gray-green, sealike expanse of our lives, following various arcs from marker to marker, circumnavigating our own personal globe from birth to death, we come to one particular buoy which seems a bit larger than the others. As we glide closer, we may notice a warm light emanating from it, leading upward and disappearing into the clouds above. Below, in the emerald water, the same light emanates, penetrating downward as far as we can see. It is a light that illuminates many events we have experienced, and bathes the face and figure of the person who has been the "significant other" in our life, the person destined to be the love of our life.

As we gaze at this light, we see that it starts at a certain place. If we study that place, we see that it is, in fact, the place and time where we first met this beloved person. Now is the time for us to describe our meeting with this one who has continued to illuminate our life ever since.

This may sound rather romantic to some of you,

even mystical, perhaps even quite unrealistic if your marriage(s) or relationships have not been happy. But this is the time to put aside old and new wounds, a time to return to that point in life where the white light of love was clear, where hope, beauty, and awe were evident, and a path into the future began to open up.

If that path ultimately became too steep to continue, strewn with boulders too large to climb over, too misty to follow, or too straight and narrow for comfort, these difficulties need not obscure the brilliance of the light or the special qualities in your beloved which the light of love first illuminated. Here is such a story.

SOME DAYS THE BIRD SINGS
by Lucy MacDougall

I'm watching a young man on stage left, something electric about him. He's wearing Lederhosen, which reveal fine sturdy legs. I've never noticed a young man's legs before. Hmmm. Attractive. I steal peeks. I stare. Brown hair, strong voice, intense eyes. Sensitivity, will, strength—they come down to me in the audience twenty feet away.

I'm sitting with two girlfriends in the auditorium of the YWCA at Lexington Ave at 53rd Street where a rehearsal of *Autumn Crocus* is going on.

"The place is jumping with guys," whispers one of my friends.

"I *see* one," I agree, fixing my eyes on him again. I'm glad my friend talked us into going to this acting group. The past few weeks I've been complaining about being twenty-two, getting old, wanting a husband and children, and wanting to find a nice guy.

After the rehearsal, we talk with some of the cast, and someone invites us to go to the Blarney Stone across the street, where everyone hangs out after rehearsals. The one I noticed with the great eyes is at the end of the table in a rumpled baggy old tweed suit now, but after an hour he hasn't even looked my way.

A guy named Jack, who's been hanging around me, points him out to me. "Have you met my buddy Ranald yet?"

Are his eyes hazel? I wonder. I can't be sure because he still won't look at me. "Hi," I say. "Glad to meet you."

He barely speaks to me, goes back to ignoring me.

What is with this guy? I think. Why doesn't he like me? Oh, who cares? I do. I can hardly wait to see him again.

◊

Ranald is drinking coffee and I'm having tea in a coffee shop in the lower level of the RCA Building. We stare at each other, the air between us crackling with electricity and energy. It's not necessary to say anything, but two people can stare for only so long.

We're not just staring. We're also taking each other in. I see he's not that handsome, he's kind of shabby and plain in his ways. His socks don't even match. He's wearing that old tweed suit that I first saw him in eight months ago at that rehearsal, and has only the skinniest trench coat I've ever seen to protect him from cold weather. But the eyes and manner are determined.

What does he see when he looks at me? I don't know. Pretty? Fun? A promise of being gentle and pliable? Maybe, but I'm sure he doesn't know who I am, because I don't myself.

"Jack told me he wouldn't be seeing you any more."

"Yes, that's true," I say.

"I couldn't ask you out before because Jack is my best friend."

What a gentlemanly way to act. I like that, but meantime he's been avoiding me for all these months. I've been playing with him right now in *Squaring the Circle* and he's never looked at me once the scenes are over.

"Are you a shy person?" I ask.

"Yes," he admits, but then adds, "and there were too many other guys around you."

And I'd encouraged those guys to be around, because he wasn't paying any attention to me!

"I'm a secretary, 8th floor," I tell him. "And I write poetry," I confess. "You're a writer?"

"Yep. NBC.... I lost my father a few months ago. He was sick from drinking so many years. So now I support my mother...."

"I have to support mine, too," I say. What an amazing coincidence.

"Do you have to go somewhere else?" he asks.

We eat at a little Chinese restaurant off Broadway. The air is full and golden in the dinky, dim joint. We take the subway to 42nd Street, walk to an old movie house. Up in the balcony, on hard seats, we watch *The Baker's Wife*. Ranald takes my hand and the feeling of some magic runs through me. Both our hands shift carefully, cautiously, from time to time as finger cramps and a little hand-sweat set in. Our shoulders edge toward each other.

After the movie we walk to the subway and he takes me home. At the door, I steady myself. For what? An onslaught? He surprises me. He says he'll see me tomorrow, gives me a brief kiss. It's so nice, he gives me a real one, and is gone.

◊

Ranald is mulling an idea, stretched out on our new dusty rose sofa in our new apartment. He is drinking coffee, smoking cigarettes, out of communication. He keeps throwing a bit of popcorn up in the air and catching it in his mouth, like a seal latching onto a fish. The very model of a working writer in the act of thinking.

He sits up, pulls me down beside him. "Now that you're pregnant, I think you should give your notice at work," he says.

"Why so soon?" After all I think, most of my salary supports my mother.

He explains that the wives of our friends aren't working any more. Each is home taking care of her baby and her husband.

"I don't want my wife working either," he adds, "I'd love you home, taking care of me, and later the baby. But . . . the thing is your mother will have to come live with us."

Was he crazy? "My *mother?*"

"Yes, otherwise we can't afford to take care of her."

How can he bring up a subject like that when we are enjoying such a good life, the happiest I've ever been. Life is about perfect right now. And who wants her listening to our sex life?

I feel guilty. I don't know if I love my mother, but I certainly don't like her. Never have. Wait a minute, how about asking his mother, who also has to be taken care of? No, the reason he doesn't want her is that he doesn't seem able to talk to her.

"We can't have kids and support two mothers," he goes on. I am figuring it up in my head myself. My mother needs about a hundred a month over the money my father, long divorced, has always sent her toward her rent.

"I'll be making a lot of money someday," Ranald says with conviction, "but we need some right now."

My eyes meet Ranald's. My heart feels like a heavy sackful of old auto parts. I hate the idea, but I can see we have to do it. Anyway, he isn't angry about it. I hate it when he gets angry.

I put on a fresh pot of coffee to perk for him. We sit a while and I stare at those little corn kernels at the bottom of the bowl that never do pop like the others. Somehow they remind me not only of my mother, but of me, too, which is worse.

I hear Ranald on the phone, not wasting a minute. "How about moving in with us?" She doesn't take a second before there comes a happy squeal through the phone. As he speaks, there are more happy sounds. She is overjoyed. This is going to snap her right out of the depression she's been in since I married. That makes me mad. Of course she said yes. I've known all along she would. She's 46 and doesn't want to go back to work anymore.

Even with all the overflowing blessings of being married, life doesn't seem quite so perfect anymore.

And there's so much more . . . .

◊

That's just the beginning. We move to Connecticut with my mother and the baby. The following year we move back to Manhattan with a new baby. The marriage goes up and down. He begins to get assignments in California, at first in radio, then with a studio. We move to California, his success growing. We move to a big house in the country outside Los Angeles and have a third child but we are once more in situations we couldn't handle years before in Connecticut. Lifestyles, values, we still can't hack the differences.

For years we've told each other over and over again what we're not, and neither of us has been able to listen. He responds with more rages that affect us all, me more withdrawing, finally nothing works. He leaves three times. The fourth time it's for good and it's fifteen years.

When he leaves I see that it's almost like the time I first set eyes on him. He wouldn't look at me then. He won't look at me now, only this time he's not shy, but terribly angry.

He marries again. He holds onto his private angers tighter and tighter. He dies of a sudden heart attack.

◊

That was seventeen years ago. I still feel puzzled at the strange mystery of why love didn't work, and left us instead with our children, our lessons, our losses. Did we have to lose whatever it was we had? Is there any way it could have been different? I've given it thought for many years, but now I can say, "I don't think so."

◊ ◊ ◊

Lucy does a number of things worth noting in this story. First of all, there are some very nice, very vivid images: "My heart feels like a heavy sackful of old auto parts." Also, she picks an appropriate place to enter each scene, starting with action or dialogue while setting the stage for us a bit before going on.

Lucy's story also has an arc. It doesn't try to tell the whole relationship, but it does tell of a beginning, a middle, and an end. It is far easier to see the path that has unfolded if we begin to create arcs, that is, a number of vivid moments put together in some pattern. In fact, the pattern is already there; it is our job as writers to uncover it.

◊ ◊ ◊

Find for yourself that most comfortable of places, perhaps get out that photo album, put on the record player one of your favorite "oldies," and re-create that first meeting. Write it **now.**

◊ ◊ ◊

Once you have written about your first meeting, you may wish to continue with other stories and incidents which tell of the ups and downs of your relationship with this very special person.

If the relationship ultimately came to an end, through divorce or death, you may wish to link the various episodes together so that the character and qualities that made this person so fascinating to you are traced from the beginning to the end of your relationship. You may even show how these same qualities may have been responsible for its termination.

What I really find touching in Lucy's story is the way she is willing to recollect the early and very special moments of her relationship to Ranald, before it went sour. Recollecting the very best in those whom we have loved is important to our later lives.

In my own case, my former wife, the mother of my two children, and I have kept alive an affection for each other and have allowed a firm friendship to grow out of the ashes of our failed marriage. Part of it is her willingness to recollect for herself and the kids the whimsical way we romanced, reminding them of the good times we had, planting in them the idea that they are the children of parents who have cared about and enjoyed each other throughout life whether divorced or not.

If you have had several marriages or relationships, each important relationship deserves to be treated in a new story, as if you two were meeting for the first time.

In the episode on trauma we dealt with the need for honest observation, and the same is true for stories of life with your beloved. No matter how the story ends, the stresses and strains of a continuing relationship deserve an honest portrayal.

Viewing your relationships from the perspective of your first meetings may help you to recapture the bright light of idealized love as you first experienced it. You may find you have reached a fuller, deeper level of feeling, or you may have reached a place of boredom and stagnation. Perhaps the retelling may open some possibilities for a better relationship. Perhaps you have reached a point of agonizing and bitter cynicism about the future of this relationship and all others. Whatever your situation, it deserves to be recorded unclouded by your changing feelings about that person. Each phase of life deserves to be seen accurately for what was or is there at a certain time.

If you are ready, go ahead and write about those other significant moments in this relationship. Be honest, fair, and open. That is all you, your audience, or your loved ones can ask of you. "He" or "she" would want you to open up. No loyalties are being violated; most of the people who will read or hear what you are composing have had similar experiences. Sharing those experiences will help others release, relieve, and unburden themselves.

◊ ◊ ◊

So go ahead. You are starting at the source of the shaft of light. You have done a good job of telling the story of your first meeting. If the path looks rocky, so be it; describe that rocky path. We will all profit from it. Get comfortable, and go on.

CHAPTER FOURTEEN

KIDS, KIDS, KIDS—
AND PARENTS TOO

A S WE REVIEW OURSELVES, CHARTING FIRST ONE course and then another across the sometimes calm, sometimes turbulent sea of life, it becomes time for us to review our lives with our offspring. Begin by listening to and savoring the sounds of that word, off-spring. Spring, as in a source of fresh water, or a leap from one place to another.

There are two things to consider when listening to the echoes of our children's voices. First, we will want to recollect the significant moments in our children's lives and the feelings we experienced then. Our children, in all likelihood, will have different feelings and recollections, and they may even wish to record their own versions of the events.

The second thing we may wish to do is describe the way in which we, as parents, related to our children and grandchildren—what we hoped to accomplish and what we did accomplish in having and raising our off-spring. We may also wish to talk about the character and qualities we see in our children and grandchildren, and relate these qualities to those of their parents and grandparents. This is important because at one time or another in our lives we are searching for our identity. To find certain traits in ourselves and see how they relate to our ancestors can be quite helpful.

One suggestion: It may be best, when describing one's children's fundamental qualities, to use positive terms which can help to inspire them in that direction. The intertwined lives of children and parents are filled with comical, touching, powerful moments.

After describing some of these, we may wish to go deeper, to reflect upon moments when our relationship changed, for better or worse. Maybe we as a parents made a decision that had a significant positive result, or maybe we failed to make an important sacrifice at an equally critical moment. If we were responsible for a failure, now is the time to own up to it. Our children may not have forgiven us, but forgiveness may be closer than we think. Or our children may have done something which hurt us, and now is a good time to get it out in the open. Not as a complaint, but as an honest story.

Of all the writing tasks my students have undertaken, writing about one's children seems to be the most difficult. Why is this so? I ask. They answer that for the most part their relationships with their children are unresolved and therefore very difficult to put into words. As we continue to discuss the issue of parent/children relationships, however, another explanation begins to surface. Many of my older adult students feel their children do not know who they are. "My children see me as a parent," says Bess. "Or as a person who was defined and labeled long ago," adds Gina. My sons and I have discussed this and my younger son agrees he has been inclined to see me as the father who he knew when he was about twelve—quick-tempered, insistent, invasive of privacy. Hopefully, I'm not so much this way now, many years later.

However, for children who leave home at eighteen for college and careers, and are no longer around much, it is hard to see changes. It is even harder to call a halt to defining those whom one has known a lifetime and ask, "Who is this person whom I have known so long?"

My older adult students are divided about whether or not this circumstance ought to be changed. Many feel it is easier to allow their children to see and remember them as the children wish; other's feel they want very much for their children to know them as they really are now. An interesting discussion of this issue took place in one of my classes and is available on videotape for those who are interested [Videotape #2, listed at the back of this book].

Writing about our children aids in the process of getting them to know who we are. Having them read our efforts to record and define our relationship to them often stimulates a great deal of discussion, some of it painful. It will probably help if we make it clear to them that there are no immutable truths to be found in our stories about them, that our writing is only our version of the truth and that we welcome their version as well.

The first of the following stories is a good example of one mother's effort to try to understand "what went wrong." The second is a very honest and poignant example of a father's efforts to have a relationship with his daughter.

There's No Word for It

by Laura Green (pseudonym)

"Mama, Tim and I are moving in together. My friend Ella and her old man will share the rent with us. That way we can afford a Venice apartment near the beach."

Beth and I are having a light lunch on this

Saturday visit. My head whirls. "Ella's father is moving in with you?" I ask.

My daughter laughs. "Oh, mother, 'her old man' means her boyfriend, 'his old lady' means his girl-friend."

This clarification doesn't stop my head from whirling nor my stomach from churning. I really don't like Tim. I recall the first time I met him at one of his acting "gigs," as he called them. He was paid a small fee and given a free dinner. Beth and I bought our own meals. As he was enjoying his large sundae dessert I could see my daughter drooling. The bastard didn't even offer her any. Am I prejudiced because he's an unemployed actor? I don't think so. That's not his fault. Acting jobs are hard to get. I'm annoyed with him because he doesn't try to earn money to supplement the few acting jobs he gets. Beth waits on tables, models, or cleans houses in order to be a dancer. Why the hell can't he?

My thoughts are interrupted. I hear my husband Harold bringing in the groceries. As I put the groceries away, Beth is telling him the news. I can see he feels as I do. His ruddy complexion is white.

Over our dessert we try to convince our daughter to change her plans. Her answer is simple. "I'm nineteen and I know what I'm doing."

I'm not sure she knows what she's doing. But I might as well accept Tim if that's what she wants. Maybe it will work out. Maybe. Feeling like a hypocrite, I ask Beth, "How can we celebrate this occasion?"

Harold chimes in. "That's a good idea. We'll invite some young friends."

"It's not necessary," Beth says, shrugging her shoulders.

We finally agree on a trip to Disneyland with a

few young friends. Our party arrives there for lunch that weekend. There's laughter and hilarity at some surrounding tables. Not at ours.

Fourteen-year-old Janet, a friend's younger sister, asks, "What is this party for?"

I'm in a quandary. I'm uncomfortable about telling such a young girl that my daughter and Tim are going to live together. So I blurt out, "We're celebrating because Beth and Tim are engaged."

We all turn to the young couple. Tim stands up. He's over six feet tall and towers over me. He looks furious. Beth stands next to him and holds his hand.

Tim splutters, "We're leaving. You . . . you go your way and we'll go our own."

Before I have a chance to find out why they are angry they both stalk out. I'm bewildered. What did I say that was so wrong? I can't wait to get home. I never did like Disneyland. I hate it now.

The next evening I call my daughter. "What was that Disneyland disaster all about? Why did you disappear? It was so hurtful to your father and me—and damn impolite to our guests."

"You had no right to announce our engagement," asserts Beth. "We're just going to live together. We're not thinking of marriage."

I'm not sure I heard right. "You mean you protested because I used the wrong word? Do you have a word to describe when you move in with your lover—I mean your 'old man'?"

"Mom, you just don't understand. It's not the word. We have a different way of living."

"Beth, I may be old fashioned but I'm not prudish. I've no objection to your moving in with someone you love, if you're committed to one another. And I just don't think Tim is good enough for you. I may not understand your lifestyle but I do understand when people are rude and unkind." I hang up.

I'm upset. "Don't lose your sense of humor," I tell myself. Instead of stalking out of the party, why didn't they just say, "This is not an engagement party. It's a non-commitment party."

Better yet, why did I suggest a celebration in the first place? Why didn't I keep my mouth shut in Disneyland?

◊ ◊ ◊

This story gives us a clear picture of the difficulty of communicating across generations. It starts with a strong beginning, "Mom, Tim and I are moving in together"—a line of dialogue which causes us to ask,"What is going to happen? How will Laura handle it?" The first line gets us on track and keeps us moving along with lots of dialogue which gives us insights into Beth, impulsive, forward-looking, impatient; Tim, dynamic, self-centered; and Laura, well-meaning, confused, and a little klutsy.

SOME VACATION

by Max Levin

I left Monday, the 16th of October, for Santa Cruz. I stopped at Harris Ranch for a steak lunch and read the paper leisurely. I had to take this vacation as a leave of absence from my job as I had made a little too much money for Social Security. Anyway, first stop to visit my daughter, Anya, in Santa Cruz.

I arrived around 5 P.M. The door was open with a little note: "Dad—am in school, will be back at six—make yourself comfortable." Gabriel, one of her roommates, greeted me. "How about a cup of coffee?"

He made me a cup and said, "I'm going to pick up Christie."

"Fine. I'll take you all to dinner tonight."

"Wonderful. The girls will love it!"

I brought my bags in, and sat on the couch reading a book I had brought along.

Anya came in. We kissed. "Had a good trip?"

"Yes. I drove at between 60 and 70. I was in no rush, took about six hours without the stops."

She made herself a cup of coffee and sat opposite me at the table. "Dad, I have to ask you something."

"Sure, go ahead . . . "

"Why did you come?"

I looked at her. What kind of question was that? "Anya, I haven't seen you since June. I had to take this vacation. I wanted to see you."

"You know no other parents come to visit their kids like this. You forced yourself on me."

I couldn't believe what I heard. "Anya, I called you several weeks ago. And you said I could stay with you a couple of days."

"You didn't ask me whether you could come— you just said you're coming."

I got up from the table. I couldn't believe this conversation. Should I take my bags right now and leave? Anger and shock were mixing in my veins and shooting to my head. I went to the other room and shut my eyes. "Max, relax, take some deep breaths," I told myself. "Is this the work of my ex-wife?"

Gabriel and Christie came in. Christie came up to me. I kissed her on both cheeks. "I'll just take a shower." She turned to Anya. "Your dad is taking us all to dinner. Isn't that lovely?"

Anya said, "Wonderful."

We went to a fish shanty on the pier. We all ordered different dishes and I ordered a nice California fumé blanc. We tasted all our choices around the table. The wine produced some good conversation. Even Anya loosened up and I felt better.

Tuesday the 17th, the next morning, was beautiful. The sky was blue. The sun was out. It was going to be a warm day.

"Anya, want to take a walk at the beach?"

"Okay, Dad—I'll be ready in ten."

For a while we walked silently at a brisk pace, and then she started again. "You know, Dad, we really have no relationship. You think we were a family, but we weren't. I know Mother, but I don't know you."

I couldn't believe all this. I said, "Anya, I was always around when you or Nicky needed me. We always went on vacation together—Canada, Oregon, New York. You kids worked with me in the restaurant. You knew exactly what I was doing all the time."

She hammered away, and I exploded. The anger took over and instead of saying, "Anya, you're making me very angry," out came, "You little cunt, you're acting just like your mother." At that moment I couldn't believe what had come out of my mouth.

"You're a chauvinist pig."

"I'm sorry, Anya, I said this." I turned and walked back. We had walked a few miles to the end of the boardwalk.

We had a make-it-yourself lunch. Christie asked Gabriel to drive her to the doctor. Anya said she would visit her friend Carla. "What are you going to do, Dad?"

"Maybe I'll go to the mall and window shop—the bookstore . . . café . . . "

"See you later."

I went to my car and suddenly thought, what did I need to go to the mall for—and shop for what?

I decided instead to take my book and go to the beach. It was calming, sitting and reading. Shortly before 5 P.M. I walked back toward the house.

Suddenly there was a tremor. The earth started dancing. I fell against a mailbox pole and held on as the pavement seemed to roll like waves. For a moment I thought the earth would open up and swallow me—the end of all my problems. A chimney of a building a couple of feet away broke off and shattered bricks, just missing me. It seemed to last a long time. Thirty seconds seemed endless. And then people ran out of their homes, looked around and called to each other: "That was a powerful quake." "Any damage in your place?" "Glasses and crystal broken." "I hope nothing happened to my husband, he should be back." A bike rider whizzed by screaming, "I'm leaving California!"

I continued quickly my way back to the house. I started to worry about Anya. Gabriel and Christie were in front of the house in each other's arms. "Oh, good, you're all right, we were worried about you."

"What about Anya?" I asked. "I tried to call Carla, but the phone doesn't work," said Gabriel.

Neighbors came by. "There is a fire, see the smoke? It looks like near 17 . . . "

And then the blue Volkswagen station wagon drove up with Anya emerging. I felt like running up to her and embracing her. But something held me back.

She seemed relieved to see me there, together with Gabriel and Christie. "It was scary," she said. "Carla's furniture got thrown all over. We held onto each other under the door frame. It took forever driving back. Some streets are ripped open. The car radio said the mall was pretty badly shaken."

The electricity was off. Gabriel brought the

portable radio. With the news coming from all directions. Then Gabriel and Christie looked for candles. By candlelight we sat around the table, munching on bread and cheese. More news.

Anya tried to call her mother in San Francisco, but the phone was dead. The bad new about the Bay Bridge and Nimitz Highway came over the airwaves. Aftershocks rumbled the earth. For moments we were silent.

Then Anya said, "It looks like you won't be able to leave tomorrow." I didn't like her tone. I said, "I'll try to leave as soon as possible—as soon as I can call my friends in Pacifica." I did want to get away as fast as possible. I didn't sleep well. More tremors about 4 A.M.

In the morning the phone started ringing. Nicky called. He was fine. Mother was all right. Christie's mother called. I tried to call Pacifica, but the lines were dead to call out.

The kids decided to walk through town to the mall to look at the damage. Anya asked, "You want to come with us?"

We walked on the promenade. The Pacific looked calm. Houses had toppled chimneys, trees blocking driveways. Toward the mall we could see houses moved from their foundation. Streets with gaping holes. People were taking pictures with their cameras.

Gabriel and Christie walked holding hands. Anya next to them. She didn't walk with me. I followed behind.

The mall was cordoned off. Crumbled buildings, crushed cars. We got the first newspaper: The *San Jose Mercury News* with a twelve page special earthquake section. We learned two people had been killed in the mall. The biggest temblor since 1906. The epicenter here, Santa Cruz.

Back at the house we found the electricity on again. The landlord came in with a cup of soap water and checked the gas lines. No leaks. I finally was able to reach my friends in Pacifica. They said Highway One to Pacifica was clear, there was no damage in Pacifica, and I was welcome.

I packed my bags, went into Anya's room. She was lying on her futon reading. She looked up.

I said, "I'm leaving to see Ken and Carol. They said there's no damage to the highway in their direction." I took a fifty dollar bill out of my billfold and dropped it on the futon. "Here's a contribution for your film work for school!"

"I don't want your fucking money. You always think you can buy me with money and gifts. Take your damn money and goodbye."

She threw it at me. I picked it up, took my bags, and walked to the car. Gabriel and Christie came out and said goodbye. Then I saw Anya appear in the doorway.

"Goodbye, Dad."

"Goodbye, Anya."

After driving a few miles out of Santa Cruz, I stopped near the beach. Slowly tears came into my eyes. Sobs. I let it all come out for a little while. I felt better. I drove on.

◊ ◊ ◊

Here is a story filled with irony: the split in the earth around Santa Cruz causes him to feel it in his soul. The earth shakes around him and inside him.

In the story he begins with action, followed by narrative and dialogue. Little by little his inner thoughts and feeling begin to surface. Sparse dialogue reveals a great deal—a resentful daughter, "Why did you come?"; a vulnerable parent, "I haven't seen you since June . . . I wanted to see you . . . you said I could stay with you."

The dignity of Max's story is in his simple, puzzled vulnerability. We feel his pain without sentimentality, without blame, simply cracks in the earth and in his soul.

◊ ◊ ◊

One caution: There is a special trap in describing one's children. It is called sentimentality, which is waxing ecstatic about how wonderful they are long before the reader or listener has a chance to know them as people. It is better to be as objective as possible, letting different situations and the way the children dealt with them delineate their character. Then it is appropriate to write about how you felt, after the event. Of course, if the event is one in which your feelings changed progressively, from concern to fear to terror, or from amusement to laughter to hysteria, then it is appropriate to write about how you felt as the event was unfolding.

There is one question you should ask yourself before you undertake to write about your children, otherwise you will certainly confront it after you start: Are you ready to write about them? Give the question some thought. When the issue of writing about children was raised in our life story writing classes, we found that many people were reluctant to express their feelings about them, primarily, they said, because the separation which inevitably occurs between parents and children requires rebonding as part of the healing process, and for many parents that rebonding had not yet occurred. Many were engaged in writing not about their children, but about their parents, and this, too, was part of the process: To be able to clear the air with your children, you need to have cleared the air with your parents. So, if you have not already done so, take this opportunity to address Mom and Dad once and for all. You may want to do this in the form of a letter to one or both of them.

A loving and moving example of this is Louis Doshay's letter, "Mom" (page 216).

◊ ◊ ◊

Now sit back in your easy chair, and go back to where the stories of your children all began, perhaps where conception actually took place ....

CHAPTER FIFTEEN

LOVE
IN LATER LIFE

IN "FIRST LOVE" WE LOOKED AT THE FIRST GLIMPSE OF love we have when we are young and our feelings surge within us and we imagine the object of our affection to be one and the same with the fantasies we have of him or her.

We have also looked at another kind of love in "The Love(s) of Your Life." Here a person of significance enters your life and rocks your boat. Your life changes because of him or her. You begin to learn life's lessons and may enter into a lengthy, enduring relationship with this significant person.

Now it is time to look at love of another kind—love in later life.

We are just beginning to recognize in our society that love of a very passionate kind is possible at any and every age. In my classes there are numerous people who have forty- and fifty-year relationships that are vigorous, growing, and evolving. A number of other people in my classes have only found their true love late in life and had never been truly happy until this person finally came along. One such story is the meeting between Don and Inge Trevor, described in "The Ad" (see page 220).

Here is another wonderful story of love later in life.

A GREEN-EYED MONSTER

by Lily Tokuda

"Get your hands off my husband!" I scream silently at Miiko as I stare at Tadd and Miiko walking ahead of me. Miiko-san drove us for miles from Hiroshima City looking for a restaurant she picked in the mountains of Yamaguchi Prefecture. This place is lit up like day and there is a complex of restaurants in the huge castle-like building with a tall white tower gleaming against the dark night.

I feel a fine mist. Though it's a lovely spring night, I feel cold. Miiko-san, a divorcee, is a daughter of our friend Izue-san. Now we are walking around smelling lovely smoky barbecued teriyaki meat and other exotic Japanese food from the various restaurants.

Miiko-san hangs onto Tadd's arm and Izue-san is holding onto mine. My stomach hurts, no, I guess it's really my heart that's aching. I try to act nonchalant. After all, Tadd and I have a wonderful marriage, all 46 years of it. Tadd loves me and he is good to me but I cannot help noticing many Japanese women, young and old, are fascinated by him. He is attractive, so different from the Japanese men who treat their women as their inferior. And they don't dress as sporty and smart as Tadd.

Tonight he is dressed in a pair of jeans and has a black windbreaker on over a light blue golf shirt. Izue-san is chattering and I can barely hear her because my ears are ringing—or is that my heart?

I swallow. My mouth is dry. I need a drink of water or I need a stick of chewing gum. I need my Tadd. We go through a maze in search of a special restaurant. Miiko-san slows down. "This is the place." She stops. I don't care if this is the best or the worst place. I am not hungry.

"Ko, ko (here, here), Lili-san." Izue-san drags me by the arm to the entrance. We remove our shoes and get on the tatami floor. Tadd takes his shoes off and Miiko straightens them out. Damn it, that's my job.

I am consumed with jealousy.

We find an empty table. Tadd pats a seat next to him for me to sit. We all sit on the floor on little blue cotton pillows. I don't feel good. My smile must look sickly but Tadd doesn't notice.

This place must be popular all right. The place is jammed with young people. In fact, we, Izue-san, Tadd and I are the only old ones. Miiko-san in her designer's outfit fits right in with them.

A waitress in a blue kimono brings us menus. "The barbecued chicken and veggie sounds good," I tell Tadd since he cannot read Japanese.

"Tadd-san, you should try their Kamam-meshi, it's their specialty," Miiko-san tells Tadd in her husky voice. She and her mother pull out cigarettes. If Tadd offers to light them, I will throw up.

I look at the menu. My chest feels so tight that I cannot breathe. My mouth is still dry. I drink a little cup of hot tea our waitress pours. It's hot and scorches my mouth but I welcome the tea.

Our food comes. I don't taste anything. Izue-san keeps up her chatter, damn, damn, just leave me alone, please. Soon we are through. Tadd gets up to pay. This is our last night with them and we want to treat them.

We find our shoes among the hundreds of pairs

of shoes. As we leave, Miiko grabs Tadd and Izue-
san gets hold of my arm. I look for a bathroom. I
want to be by myself. I want to cry.

Back into the car. Tadd sits in front with Miiko-
san and Izue-san and I climb into the back. I imagine their hands touching. My gosh I am getting
paranoid. I must stop this. I must be sick in the
head.

Finally, we are home. After our customary hot
furo (bath), we bid our good night to Izue-san and
Miiko-san. "Doh-mo Arigato, it was lovely," I say.

We get into our futon. I feel cold in spite of the
thick futon. I have to talk. I have to tell Tadd how
I feel. "You know, darling, I felt real, real sad tonight."
My voice sounds strange to my ears.

"How come?" Tadd gropes for me in the darkness.

"Because I wanted to walk with you instead of
Miiko. I wanted to hold onto your arm."

"Hey, I'm old enough to be her father."

"Ha, I bet she doesn't feel that Tadd is old
enough to be her father," I say to myself. I wonder
when she lost her father.

"I love you, you know that." Tadd holds me tight
and reassures me. I smell his clean soapy smell. I
feel a little better. Not one hundred percent, but
much better. Even at my age, that green-eyed monster can still get to me. Will I be like this even when
I am in my 80s and 90s? I wonder.

◊ ◊ ◊

Lily gives us a story dense with humor and feeling.
It draws us into the experience from the very first line.
In giving us a well-balanced narrative, Lily reveals
clearly the depth of her feelings. The story also puts to
bed several stereotypes: that older adults don't have
much sexuality, and that those whose emotions are

hard to read, i.e., "inscrutable" Orientals, don't have emotions.

Stories such as these remind us that for all of us there are many unexpected twists and turns to our life's path and that we can best prepare for them by remaining optimistic about and open to whatever is coming next. The next story is an example of the kind of love that supports many a long-term relationship because it is seasoned with so much acceptance, good humor, and private resolve.

65th

by Stella Goren

"All three of them called today," my husband, Sam, tells me with a sigh.

"All three—you mean our children?" I ask. "What for?" As if I couldn't guess. Tomorrow is June 26, my birthday, and our three children have called to remind their father to get me a present. They call him before every occasion, not that it does any good. But if they should neglect to call, Sam uses it as an excuse that no one reminded him.

Sam heaves another sigh. "I never know what to get you. How about buying yourself something and tell them it's from me?"

No, Mr. Goren, I say to myself, you're not going to get off so easy this time. No presents on Mother's Day because, as you say, I'm not your mother. Valentine's Day is strictly commercial. Anniversaries we celebrate by taking the kids out to supper where they shower us with gifts. But my birthday is *my* day and this being my 65th birthday, have I got an idea for you.

To Sam, I suggest, "What if I tell you what I want and where to get it?"

He looks at me. "What do you want from my life?"

he groans. "You got your credit cards and checks. Why don't you get whatever you want?"

I shake my head. I stand fast. He sighs. "OK—what is it you want?"

I hold my head high and with no hesitation, I tell him, "A sexy negligee!"

Sam looks askance at me. I know what he's thinking, "What the hell does an old bag want with something like that?" He has said many times that such items don't faze him. His theory is: Take it off—all off.

"OK," Sam agrees. "Where do I get it?"

Looking him eye-to-eye, I respond, "Frederick's of Hollywood!" He gives me a weird look, confirming his opinion that I'm getting senile.

Next day, Sam presents me with a box from Frederick's, which I nervously open and lift out the sheerest, reddest negligee. It's the first one I've ever owned. Maybe not the one I would have picked out myself, but it means more because my husband has gotten it for me. I give him a big hug and a kiss, then ask the questions I have been visualizing all day. "How did you feel about going into that store? How did you decide which one to pick? Were you nervous?"

With his usual bravado, he answers, "Me, nervous? Nah! I just went in, picked out the first one I thought would fit."

I'm disappointed! This didn't coincide with my plan. I wanted him to sweat a little. But he had gone, and I did get my negligee.

I can't exactly "slip" into the gown that night as it fits a little snug, but the silky, filmy material feels sensual on my skin. My breasts bulge over the low-cut tight neckline; the nipples protrude uncharacteristically. I run my hands up and down my body. It feels great! The tag is still on the robe. The price is $45.00. I leave it attached, a reminder of the price of my vanity and the need to have my husband show his love.

◊ ◊ ◊

In this story, Stella balances narrative, dialogue, and inner thoughts and feelings quite effectively. She begins with crisp dialogue, drawing us into the story, then in the next few paragraphs she sets the stage, enabling us to ask: "Why does this guy need so much prodding?", "What kind of a relationship do they have?", "Will she ever get a birthday present of the kind she wants?" By the end of the story we have answers to all these questions. Her vivid dialogue gives us a very clear picture of Sam: spoiled, put-upon, unsentimental; of Stella: bemused, tolerant, wistful; and of the give and take of their very real, very believable relationship.

◊ ◊ ◊

*If this chapter on love in later life touches you in some way, reminds you of your experiences of those you love, write the moments that come to you ... **now.***

CHAPTER SIXTEEN

OUR PRESENT CONDITION AND OTHER STORIES

FLOATING GENTLY TOWARD OUR SAFE HARBOR, relaxed and somewhat detached, we take a good look at our present, where we are now. We ask ourselves if we are content with the life we have lived. What must we do to accept those parts of our lives that still make us uncomfortable? How has life changed for us, inwardly and outwardly, over the years? For some of us life, outwardly, may have changed a great deal, and it is valuable to see how our inner self has responded to those changes. At this point you might like to read one such comparison. Please turn to Anne Freedman's "Driving Miss Anne" (page 229).

There is no final, glorious landing with trumpets playing and bands marching, not on this voyage. Nor is it like Columbus opening up a route to a new continent, where millions will follow in times to come. It is our own personal, soulful voyage, expressed in our own personal terms.

But, as with any voyage, there is excitement. As we re-experience our life's journey, we begin to realize that each tack we have taken had a reason behind it, a logic of some kind, perhaps not apparent at the time. Revisiting the past, we see that there were people with whom we would like to be reunited. Our journey may help us to do this. For some of us there is the welcome realization that our later years can be very exciting. Though the body may slow and some memory functions, overloaded with stored material, act a bit erratic, that's OK; it's our renewed relationship with our deepest past that can replenish us at this point.

We can begin to write about significant experiences we have had during our mature years—trips we have taken, memorable people we have met, successes and failures, and events that we may even have helped shape and change.

PARADOX AND IRONY

One possible, frequently interesting approach to these stories is to write about the presence of unpredictability, paradox, and the unusual in our experiences. Most of us have, at one time or another, had a sense that life is or was playing a trick on us. Just as we were sure things were going to happen a certain way, they happened in exactly the opposite way.

The part played in our lives by unpredictability, paradox, and coincidence has been recognized in all cultures. In Greece and Rome, Proteus and Mercury were mythical figures of change and uncertainty; in Native American and Meso-American cultures, "trickster" figures were and remain ever-active in the mythologies. In Christianity, the devil is often seen as having some trickster qualities, as we can see in the phrase, "The devil made me do it." During the Renaissance in Italy, the goddess Fortuna was recognized as embodying the paradoxical fates which may befall one at any time.

"Tricky," unpredictable qualities may also exist in

ourselves, and may come out at unusual times, leading to fun, frustration, bewilderment, or defeat. So, you might try writing stories that reveal contradictions, paradoxes, and ironies in you and your life. Some of these qualities of paradox and irony are to be found in Selma Lewin's "You Can't Always Go Home Again" (page 233). Other stories may deal with unexplained and unpredictable actions and occurrences which ultimately give rise to a fascination with how varied, mysterious, and even magical life can be.

THE VOYAGE TO THE OTHER SIDE

In a sense, these stories become a preparation for another, final voyage, the one beyond our present condition. If we are shut off from our past and present, with few friends and relatives around us, then the final voyage may threaten us as terrifying and lonely, a mirror of our present condition. Or it may offer us an escape, a desperate retreat into the unknown, as if anything might be better than the present. For those who are sick and disabled this may, in fact, seem to be a very positive alternative.

Yet, if we have prepared ourselves properly, if our love relations are intact, our dependents freed, the painful and unfulfilled parts of ourselves accepted, our life's experiences understood, accepted, and passed on to generations to come, then our present condition can be a positive experience and the final voyage can be its ultimate peak.

From the reports of people who "died" and then actually returned to life—revived drowning victims, recovered surgery patients, and the like—we sense more and more clearly the existence of a life beyond our material one. As we develop a better understanding of the zone between the two worlds, we need to think about how we will prepare for whatever is "out there."

Turn now to the story on page 237, a provocative, poetic narrative by E.S. called "First Days." In the story he asks us to climb into the coffin with an all-too-recently departed loved one and to share his journey beyond. What we see is this: The past and the dead have an enormous grip on the present and on the living. E.'s character, outward bound on the final voyage, asks the living to let go of those who have ceased to live in earth time so they may pursue their final journey into eternal time.

◊ ◊ ◊

*If a significant moment in your life becomes visible, a moment full of unpredictability, irony, paradox, or mystery, write it . . . **now.***

◊ ◊ ◊

Now that you have reviewed the stages of your life, you may be better able to see the directions it has taken, and how you have responded to the challenges that presented themselves at different times. Perhaps this review has enabled you to see your journey and your goal more clearly, and given you a better sense of who you are. It has probably enriched your writing as well, allowing for a deeper contact with yourself and a freer, more confident expression of your feelings.

Through writing about our life experiences, we rediscover a sense of awe about and a fascination with the unpredictability and absurdity, the joy and the mystery of the world we live in.

You will find the writing of your life's stories a fully engaging process. Give it your best effort. The time you spend may become a peak experience of your life. The more fully you dedicate yourself to writing deeply from within, the more fully your joys and sorrows will be transformed into wonderful stories for generations yet unborn to enjoy.

CHAPTER SEVENTEEN

INTERVIEWING OTHERS: ORAL HISTORY AND BEYOND

OUR EFFORTS UP TO NOW HAVE BEEN DIRECTED toward creating writers where none existed before. Many people, however, for a variety of reasons, do not want to write their own life stories, yet they are interested in having their histories recorded, or they wish to record someone else's story. The techniques of writing these kinds of stories differ from those we have used and discussed previously.

There are essentially two ways of doing this:

1. Recording your interview of the subject on audio or video tape, then transcribing the session onto paper. These are called oral histories.

2. Writing down your experience of listening to your Mom or Dad, Grandma or Grandpa, or other family member telling stories of the past, while capturing the relationship that existed between you and the storyteller at the time the story was told to you. In our life story writing classes we call these family histories.

RECORDING ORAL HISTORIES

When these life histories are recorded on video or audio tape and later transcribed onto paper, they are known as oral histories. Sometimes the oral histories are done by the subjects themselves; at other times they are done by interviewers taping family members, friends, or clients.

Whether you interview yourself or someone else, the series of questions given below will enable the persons being interviewed to reveal as much interesting information about themselves and their experiences as possible. The questionnaire is followed by a sample oral history by Nat Leventhal, as recorded, transcribed, edited, and typed by Betty Springer.

A second kind of oral history is the story "Pool Hall" by Grace Holcomb. She began by recording her ex-husband Ted Brown's life on tape; then, using the techniques described in Part I, she transformed his narrative into intense life stories using dialogue, narration, inner monologues, etc. After writing each story creatively, she checked back with him to be sure that what she had written was as close to what had happened as possible.

INTERVIEW QUESTIONS

1. What is your earliest memory?

2. What is your earliest truly strong and powerful memory?

3. Can you describe your parents, or the person(s) who raised you?

4. What were the strongest good and bad traits of your parents?

5. Do you remember any stories that illustrate these traits?

6. What is the happiest early memory you have?

7. What is the saddest or most frightening early memory you have?

8. What are some of the experiences you remember most vividly from your childhood?

9. Do you remember any friends who were particularly important to you?

10. Do you remember any interesting stories about these friends?

11. What was school like?

12. Do you remember any interesting stories about your schooling?

13. Who was the first boy (or girl) you fell in love with? What was that like?

14. Do you remember any difficult or important decisions you had to make during your early years?

15. What were some of the jobs or occupations you worked at during your life?

16. Do you remember any interesting or funny stories about your work?

17. Many times in life we remember things one way but our friends and relatives remember them differently. Do you have any experiences like this?

18. Often in life we have stories of sadness and trauma which are important to talk about. What has happened in your life that you remember with real sadness?

19. Most of us have had one person in our lives who was very important to us, a man or woman whom we have loved a great deal. Who was that person in your life?

20. What was it about that person that made him or her so special?

21. How did you meet? What were the circumstances?

22. Were there other people—teachers, counselors, friends—who helped shape your life and attitudes?

23. Who were they? What were they like?

24. Many of us have children who have given us a great deal of pleasure and pain. Would you like to describe yours?

25. Do you remember any stories that really tell something about your relationship with your children?

26. If there were one thing you would like to tell your children and those who will come after them, what would it be?

◊ ◊ ◊

The following oral history segment is a fragment from the life story of Nat Leventhal, an eighty-six-year-old former tailor who emigrated from Russia and was intimately involved with the growth of the garment industry in America from 1914 onward. He returned to Russia in the late 1920s to help Russian garment workers learn American garment industry techniques, some of which, paradoxically, he had learned in Russia as a small child.

SAMPLE ORAL HISTORIES

BECOMING AN AMERICAN

by Nat Leventhal
Interviewed and edited by Betty Springer

In July of 1914, I came to the harbor of Boston. Everything looked so different to me. The people who were working at the docks had hard straw hats and they spoke a language which I couldn't understand; it was strange to me. They didn't have quotas. They just looked at you and saw if you were healthy, then they put you on a train and sent you where you belonged.

At that time the immigrants were accepted with open arms, regardless of race, color, or whatever. Five doctors looked me over to make sure I was healthy and then I was put on a train to Chicago. My sister lived in America, and she had bought my tickets ahead of time and made the arrangements with the agent. When we got to Chicago she was waiting outside the station. There were no guards and we walked among the Americans. She recognized me and took me to her home on a streetcar.

In those years when I came, my sister had a grocery store in the front and the living quarters in the back. She had a big galley stove that used to keep us warm. We used to put coal in it and would stay around the stove. We didn't have bathtubs in the house; we went to the steam houses. We did not have toilets in the apartment. They were in the hallway and everybody got a key for the toilets. That was the life in those days, in 1914 and 1915.

In those days when you came to a place on the Loop between downtown and home you used to get a big stein of beer for five cents, then all the smor-

gasbord you could eat for free. That was those days!
When I stayed with my sister, I used to get a nickel
and we'd get pails made out of metal which would
take about fifteen glasses of beer. We used to go to
the brewery and pick up a pail of this beer on hot
days in the summer. The whole family used to
drink beer and that was our enjoyment. When we
had time on Sunday, we used to go to a park near
the lake. My sister would bring sandwiches and we
used to have a good time. We also had in Chicago
the Jewish theater, the Jewish papers. We didn't
have to use the English language so much. Most of
us used the Jewish language at home, therefore we
still retained our accent. We hadn't developed a
real American accent.

Afterwards, I was trained to be a tailor. I first
started to train when I was six years old in Russia.
In America I didn't know the language, but I read
the Jewish papers and found an ad for a man that
knows tailoring. So, I came to work early in the
morning, at seven o'clock. I did my work and at
seven in the evening, I said, "I'm going home."

"What's the matter with you, half a day?" Seven
to seven is half a day! So, I didn't want to work
there any more.

At that time there were no automobiles but
mostly horses and wagons. I used to try to learn to
jump on the streetcar, to jump on and off. That was
a trick that all the youngsters used to do. I did, too.
But one time I got dressed to visit my sister about
fifty miles away. I jumped off one street car to take
the other, and jumped wrong. I jumped straight
and fell in the mud. I was all covered with mud,
and when I went to my sister, she didn't know who
it was. Finally she recognized me. I had to change
from head to foot because I was all smeared up.

◊ ◊ ◊

This type of oral history has its advantages: simplicity and the relative ease with which the subject can tell his story. It has its disadvantages too:

First, the story is almost always told by means of uninterrupted narrative with little or no dialogue and inner thoughts used. The story is not shaped in any way. After a while, uninterrupted narrative becomes taxing, even boring for us to read. To hold our interest stories need variety and contrast.

Second, the teller of the story seldom does any rewriting of the story so the process of exploring one's own search for truth through revising is lost.

Third, stories of an event can often be well told orally, but a story involving relationships often cries out for a fuller and deeper treatment of the experience using dialogue, inner monologue, and attention to form. But where the storyteller does not wish to or cannot go into more depth, this type of oral history is viable and interesting.

◊ ◊ ◊

The second type of oral history integrates "writing from within" techniques into the oral history narrative. The first step in this process is to record one's own story or that of a friend or relative on a tape recorder. Then, using the techniques described in Part I, the oral narrative can be transformed into a series of separate stories which stand on their own. An example of this second type of oral narrative is "Pool Hall," a story from the life of Ted Brown as told to and written by his former wife, Grace Holcomb. "It all started with those tapes," she says. "We got him a six pack, cracked it open, hit 'record' and let Ted go. The story I wrote might have been just a few lines on tape. I just took it from there."

"Often times," she says, "what I did creatively might not have been accurate but it got him to remember what *did* happen." She adds fondly, "It's all up there in that thick skull of his somewhere. I just had to shake it loose somehow." With his input, she made changes, then brought the story to class, listened to more comments, reworked it, showed it to Ted one last time, revised again, and finally had a story. Here is an excerpt from one such story.

POOL HALL

Story by Ted Brown
Written by Grace Holcomb

Our town, Collbran, Colorado, only had about 300 or so people in the 1930s while I was growing up, and we had the usual assortment of stores in town.

By and large, the very best place in town to kids was the one and only pool hall. We loved it. As pool halls go, it wasn't much. Just a large room, with a couple of big windows, usually dirty, and an inside toilet, one of the few we had. There was a bar all along one side of the room and beer and whiskey were sold, but not too much whiskey. Mostly everybody was a beer drinker. But, if you wanted to just nurse a bottle of whiskey in private there were five or six tables and chairs. Men would just sit with the whiskey and a shot glass; they always drank it neat, and everybody knew enough to leave them alone. If they wanted company, they would sit at the bar. The tables were mostly used for playing cards. The men played pinochle and pitch during the day and poker at night.

The pool hall was where the cowboys headed when they got paid and were in town to tie one on. Those poor bastards worked like dogs and pretty much lived like dogs too. They only got to town once a month when they got paid.

But the pool hall meant more to us than cowboys. Old Dewey Fitzpatrick hung around there too. He was an old man, must have been 50 or so, and he would spin stories for us.

"Dewey, please tell us again about how you lost your fingers?" we'd plead. "Well," Dewey would say, "sure you boys can take a bloody tale?" "Oh, yes, sir," we would answer. "You ain't agonna tell your mammas I done gave you bad dreams, are you?" he asked. "Oh, no, sir," we answered in chorus.

He then proceeded to tell us how he was fighting bears and this one bear was extra special mean. Dewey beat off the bear, of course, but just for damned orneriness the bear jumped up and bit off the ends of two of his fingers. He would then hold them up for us to inspect.

That old dope would go on telling stories about skinning buffalo and fighting Indians. We figured some of his stories could be true, he sure was old enough.

He just did odd jobs around town, and was the town drunk if he could afford it, but he always had time to spin a tale or two for us, and they were never quite the same except for the bear and the fingers. He never changed that story. He'd tell us about being in the middle of a buffalo herd and a whole company of Indians came at him. "But, Dewey," we would protest, "last time it was only a few Indians." "Well, hell, boys, think that only happened once? This was a different time," he said. "Shut up now, and listen or I ain't gonna tell you no more." We would all be quiet because you never knew what he was going to say each time.

One time Dewey was in the pool hall, pretty drunk, and went into the toilet. Fred Wallace wanted to go in the toilet and old Dewey wouldn't get off the pot.

Fred was the son of Bill Wallace, one of the biggest and richest ranchers around that area, and Bill Wallace was one of the meanest sons-of-bitches we had. He was built and looked like a pit bull and his son Fred was just like him. Fred was about twenty when he was trying to get Dewey out of the toilet and it made him madder than hell. The other men heard the commotion in the toilet, but by that time it was too late.

Dewey was dead. Fred had dragged him off, then hit him so hard Dewey's head hit on the edge of the toilet bowl, killing him instantly.

Poppa was constable at that time, so he told us this story. Poppa came and told Fred to go on home —he would decide what was to be done later.

We had no courthouse or judge in Collbran, so Poppa and Fred drove into Grand Junction. Bill, Fred's father, was already in Grand Junction. Poppa came home the same day and so did Bill and Fred.

Poppa never did say what happened, and I never knew. All he would say was "Well, you know Bill Wallace has a lot of influence around here."

The town was pretty well divided over whether Fred should have gone to jail, but with time, it was forgotten. But the little boys of the town, of which I was one, never forgot it. We all wished we were bigger—we wanted to hang Fred ourselves. We all wanted to be the one to tie the noose. We missed old Dewey. He had been our friend. The pool hall was never quite the same with Dewey gone.

◊ ◊ ◊

WRITING FAMILY HISTORIES

Many of us who set out to write life stories are primarily interested in writing about the struggles and history of our parents and grandparents. "I want to tell my children about my parents and grandparents before it is too late," they say. Typically this kind of story is a simple narrative retelling of the past much like Nat's oral history.

> My grandfather was born in the Ukraine. When he was 16 he was forced to serve in the Czar's army. After a year he escaped and made his way to America . . . .

While reading this sort of narrative, we, the readers, find ourselves asking a number of questions: How did the narrator hear about his grandfather? Who told him the story? How do we know it is true? How did the people involved (Grandpa and the narrator) feel about these events?

Out of a need to answer these questions, another, more authentic way of telling family histories has emerged, one in which the feelings of both the story-teller and the writer are evident while the story is unfolding.

"When writing this kind of family history," I tell my students, "let the reader know how you learned about the story." Were you sitting on Grandma's knee or taking a walk with Grandpa? Let the reader know what you remember Grandpa or Grandma doing or feeling while he or she is telling you the story. That way we get both the story and your relationship to the storyteller. We will believe it and feel it more fully. Lucy MacDougall's "Family History" is a good example of this kind of writing.

FAMILY HISTORY
by Lucy MacDougall

My mother was dozing after lunch when I got to her room in the nursing home. Three nickels she won at Bingo were still in her lap. She woke right up at the prospect of an Eskimo Pie and her weekly copy of the *National Enquirer,* which she has told me at this point in her life she enjoys more than the Bible.

"How have you been?" I asked. "Fine," she said. At death's door, in the grip of gray depression or desperation, my mother always said fine.

I sat on the edge of her bed, scanning the state of her health in the wheelchair for myself as she bit into the chocolate covering. Would I be like that in 25 years, with occasional spurts of spirit and energy, living days the size and shape of postage stamps?

Her gaze, though, was intent still. She'd gobbled the Eskimo Pie while I was staring at her. Now she was staring at me, impatient, ready to get on with it. I picked up my pencil and paper in a hurry.

"I was my father's favorite," she said right away.

My mother had been waiting patiently for days while I poked around in the past for her immediate ancestors. Now she was looking forward to being born and getting on with her own personal first-hand memories. Three other babies had to be born first. "Edward came first," she said, "then Albert and Percy, and I came next." Her mother named her Irene Jeannette Scherrer. 1883. The first girl.

Her face suddenly clouded. I knew. It was going to be about Percy. It was always sad about Percy. Little Percy got sick with diphtheria and my grandmother and the housekeeper took care of him, but it was while Grandma was at work that he died. "Your Grandma would never go back to work after that. She took care of us and did piecework at home. Percy was her favorite," she explained.

"But I was my father's favorite," my mother said again, anxious to make herself once more the rightful star of her own story. "Much more than Roma."

Here comes Roma, upsetting the order of the years. Here she comes, pushy pushy little sister, on

the scene in my mother's memory when my mother's
barely gotten herself born yet. "Just like her," my
mother said when I mentioned it, the surface of her
placidity shaken even after over eighty years by the
appearance in the family of Roma with her dark
hair, dark eyes, rosy skin, her fresh, demanding,
little-girl ways, not taking any time to be a baby in
my mother's memory.

"Eddie would ask her for a glass of water," my
mother said, "and she'd bring it to the table and
spit in it before she gave it to him."

"Wait a minute. That's later, when Aunt Roma's
a little girl. She's not born and you're not even five
yet." "I don't remember anything until then," insisted my mother stubbornly. "That's the way Roma
was. But my father liked *me* more because *I* took
after the Scherrers. They were very well-bred people, I told you that, and *I* took after that side of the
family."

So my mother didn't want to be like her mother
any more than I wanted to be like mine, or my
daughters want to be like me. She had great ad-
miration for her mother's fine qualities, but also
seemed to feel a little above her. I asked her about
this. She stirred uncomfortably. It was too late in
life to bother to lie. "Well, a little," she confessed.

But my mother absolutely hated Roma. Probably because she felt my grandma spoiled Roma.
"She let her get away with anything," my mother
complained now for the thousandth time. Since my
grandma was a gentle, quiet person, she must have
had it hard to keep Roma in line. I asked about
Roma's terrible sins. My mother's anger was good
as new. "My *shoes*," she cried. "I was saving them
for best and when I went to wear them, she'd worn
them out. And borrowing my best kid gloves from
my bureau drawer, without asking, of course, and

she *stretched them*." Roma's real sin, though, I can see, was taking center stage, struggling to take over princess position in the family.

To get her mind off Roma, I told her my memories of what she had told me in the past. The old joys softened her grievances. Wearing a mulberry satin hair ribbon on the braids of her fine hair, ruffles on the dresses her mother sewed for her, carrying her roller-skates from the hard-packed dirt of Watts Street to another Village street, Mulberry, I think, where a man with a store had put in a stretch of cement in front. Roller-skating for hours.

"I didn't go to school until I was 7. Your grandma taught me at home," she said. When she finally went to school, they put her in third grade.

"I was very smart," she said pridefully. "My brother Eddie and I learned piano. The German teacher rapped our knuckles for any mistakes. Eddie would practice for hours, but the teacher said I had more talent, even though I didn't practice." Her face warmed at the thought of being able to top the brother at something.

"Talent needs practice," I pointed out, becoming the mother. She didn't agree. "Eddie got the bicycle *just* because he was a boy. He got the camera. He went on day trips with my father. He got it all, *just* because he was a boy." She still resented it. She had to have something more and better than he did, so she'd kept the teacher's remark deep inside for years to balance the books.

She'd kept everything deep inside, that was her style. She never told Eddie or Roma or anyone in the family how she felt. "It made me sick. Roma and Eddie fighting all the time over who got what. I couldn't stand it. I'd crawl under the dining room table and hide there until it was quiet and I could come out."

Harold was the change of life baby for my grandma, a blue baby, my mother said. I remember Harold was always dear to her. I liked him, too. An agreeable moon-faced man when I was a little kid. He was born to my grandma when my mother was 12. Harold Blessing Scherrer, named after some friends of Grandma's. Grandma liked to name her children after her friends to honor long associations.

"I brought him up," my mother said proudly. "I carried him around. I fed him and dressed him and changed his diapers." She'd told me that again and again, and what a help it was to grandma, who hadn't counted on her last little blessing.

My mother got a bit confused about this now. "I had this little son, Brian. He was my little boy." "No, Mom," I said gently. "That is *my* son. He's your grandson."

"Oh. Yes. That's what I mean. It was Harold who was my son."

"No. He was *like* a son. Remember?" She shook her head. She couldn't seem to get it right. "You were 12 or 13 and he was your *mother's* baby. You took such good care of him," I added.

She averted her face. "Of course," she said, but I could tell she was embarrassed that she hadn't got that stuff straight.

She was tired. The past was pictures in her head and in mine, but it was more than that. The pictures filled our whole bodies, took them over. We were both tired.

That was enough for today.

◊ ◊ ◊

As Lucy records her mother's story, we have an opportunity to get to know several relationships: Lucy's to her mother and vice versa, her mother's to the past and Lucy's own views of her mother's sisters and brothers. The assignment was made easier for Lucy because she had recorded and noted many conversations with her mother over the years.

Notice the way the frame Lucy creates (the mother speaking to Lucy the narrator) helps us see and feel the mother's struggle to get the facts straight, and feel Lucy's patient yet amused concern for her mother.

Because Lucy's mother speaks directly to Lucy, we, the readers, experience the story through Lucy's eyes. It is important for us as readers or listeners to know through whose eyes we are experiencing events at every turn in the story. It creates belief in the story. It also increases our interest because writer and teller have a relationship to share with us, in addition to the subject matter of the story itself.

A hundred years ago we would not have thought to ask "From whose point of view are we seeing the story and is it to be believed?" Until the middle of the 19th century writers like Poe, Dana, Scott, Thackeray, Hardy, Melville and many others told their stories from a god-like or omniscient narrative point of view, and we accepted this point of view as truthful. But in the writings of Stephen Crane, Henry James, and James Joyce, and in the dramas of Pirandello, readers became more aware of the person through whose eyes the story was being experienced and seen.

So, as contemporary readers, we no longer take for granted the truth of a story unless we know something about who is telling it. By recording the relationship of the storyteller to the writer of the story, we get a more authentic and believable view of the family history that is being told.

CHAPTER EIGHTEEN

THE BENEFITS OF WRITING FROM WITHIN

HEALING FROM WITHIN

Self-healing

Writing from within ourselves, going beyond the facts and into the moment to moment feelings of our lives, can be scary but also deeply liberating. Done honestly and diligently it can help clarify our lives, allowing us to value our strengths, forgive ourselves and others for real or imagined hurts, and let go of events or people who have confused, angered, or weighed upon us. This will allow us to embrace more fully those who have given us love, support, and guidance and to look forward to that which is ahead of us.

How can we get the most from the writing from within that we have done? One way is to ask at the end of each story, "What did I learn from this experience back then? What am I learning from the experience now? What am I holding back that I could express?"

Handling loss creatively

At a certain point in our lives those we care about deeply begin to fail. Perhaps they are still living but need care we cannot provide and must be placed in an appropriate facility. Perhaps they hardly recognize us. (Perhaps that person is me or you.) The consequence is that we feel very alone. Our sense of loss affects us deeply. In many cases our sense of self-esteem is badly shaken. Often when this happens our resolve to write, our discipline is shaken. We don't want to write; we dwell on the object of our loss, excluding all else.

Writing about that special person may be difficult but it is necessary for us and for them. Writing of the sweet, happy times is good. Writing of the struggles is good, too. Writing about the absurdities and ironies of our relationship is important as well. Sometimes the results of doing this are quite surprising.

One student of mine had been having a hard time writing during the first few months of class. Her stories were short, factual, and very limited in what they revealed. When I asked her what was going on, she replied, "My husband is in the hospital with Alzheimer's disease. It's very hard to think of anything else." She was trying to avoid thinking about him by writing stories that had little to do with their relationship or about the human or humorous side of the man. He had been a prominent physician and she couldn't help but see the difference between the way he had been and the way he was when she went to visit him. "He's only conscious five minutes out of the hour," she said. "Even then, just barely."

I suggested she do the difficult thing—take the bull by the horns, write about their relationship. She was younger than he, a dutiful wife, awed by his place in the profession, content to write about the trips they had taken around the world traveling from one professional meeting to another. "Write the stories of your life together," I suggested. "The growing up years, the struggles, how absurd he could be."

She laughed. "Oh, he could be. Maybe I should write about the time he was drunk in Paris and got propositioned right in front of my eyes." The class laughed and began clapping, wanting this stuffed shirt unstuffed.

AN EVENING IN PARIS
by Helen Winer

"Show me the way to go home.
I'm tired and I want to go to bed..."

Lou is singing as we walk along the boulevard in Paris in June of 1954. He had lectured at the university that afternoon on his specialty, dermatology, and we had stopped to have some wine after his talk.

"...oh, I had a little drink about an hour ago and it went right to my head..."

Barbara, our college age daughter, has been getting more and more disgusted with her father and so she steps back to join me and her sister Marylee who is 14. Lou keeps on singing.

Just then a very pretty floozy walks up to Lou and says, "You want to come home with me?"

"No," says Lou, waving his hand toward us. "I've got my wife and daughters with me here and I'm just singing. Say," he says, looking at her face which is very close to his, "I'm going to send you to the best dermatologist in Paris. Tell him to treat you. You've got some bad-looking moles on your face. You don't want to have your pretty face spoiled by these moles, do you?" She looks at him in complete surprise. "Say Helen," he turns to me, "Do you have Jean Civatte's card in your purse? Give it to this girl." I give the card to her. "Now run along kid." He turns to me. "Come, walk with me instead of with the girls." He smiles and begins singing . . .

"Wherever I may roam, on land or sea or foam
You can always hear me singing this song . . . ."

Barbara and Marylee and I join in as we walk down the street.

" . . . show me the way to go home."

◊ ◊ ◊

The class was delighted to see a different, informal, human side of their relationship. They were pleased that she could look at this dying man, the man she loved and adored, and see his imperfections and absurdities and laugh at them even as he lay dying a few miles away.

"Take this story and read it to him," I told her.

She looked at me as if I were an idiot. "He's not conscious," she said perplexed. "He can't even speak and he can't hear anything." She shook her head, almost in tears.

"Whether he seems to be conscious or not, read it to him," I insisted. "Believe me, he'll hear it. And he'll love it. Just hold his hand. Whether he says anything or not, you'll be able to feel in his hand that he is hearing you."

"If you say so, I'll do it," she answered, unconvinced.

◊ ◊ ◊

The following week she came to class with a story of her experience at his bedside.

I READ MY STORY TO LOU

As I enter Crescent Bay Convalescent Hospital, I notice one of my friends, a patient, coming toward me in her wheelchair. "Do you wish to hear my latest story?" I ask. "My teacher said I should read it to Dr. Winer and see his reaction."

"Ya, sure. I like your stories. I'll listen even if he doesn't," says Mary "because he probably is only half here." We go into his room and he is half-awake. I start my story.

"Show me the way to go home.
I'm tired and I want to go to bed . . . "

Lou stiffens. I can see he hears my voice. I take his hand. As I read he begins to smile. By the time I read about the floozy girl who tried to pick him up, he is grinning from ear to ear. "It's OK honey, I never looked at another woman. Just you!" Lou says and then dozes off. I smile at Mary and put my story in my purse.

I go home and hug myself.

◊ ◊ ◊

From this experience of Helen's we can learn a number of things. First of all, if we have relatives or friends who are badly ill or near death, we need not give them up as lost. They may not be awake, but they are accessible. Talking to them when they are in an unconscious state will be good for them whether they seem to respond or not. Writing about an experience which has been shared, bringing back the good times of the past, and reading the moment to them rather than merely talking about it, is all the more powerful because we have taken the time and energy to shape the experience artistically.

When someone is a long way away and we intend

to make contact with him or her, we need to write the experience we wish to share. The more vividly we write, the more deeply our loved one will be touched within.

FINDING OUR AUTHENTIC WRITER'S VOICE

Writing our life's stories has given us the opportunity to approach events and experiences creatively, perhaps for the first time in our lives. We have learned that writing is not a thing so magical that only a few can do it. We can create. We can write. By softening our critic, by seeking out helpful feedback, and by becoming aware of our own process when we work, we can continue to grow as writers and storytellers. Little by little, we are discovering our own authentic voices as writers. By first looking at life through the innocent eye of the child who still dwells within us, we can write stories in a way that is fresh, direct, visual, and emotional. Our critic is at rest.

Sometimes our lives may even depend on our ability to tell a story well.

At a recent lecture I gave at UCLA, a member of the audience told me that an ESL student of his from Nicaragua, a teacher in his native country, had decided to escape, knowing that the Contras in his area were very much against teachers like himself. He swam out to sea hoping to be picked up by a fisherman but, as luck would have it, he was washed ashore and into the hands of a group of Contras. They shot him several times, but did not kill him.

Later that night as the soldiers sat around the campfire telling stories, the teacher realized his only hope of survival was to tell such interesting stories that they would begin to see him as a human being. So, despite his wounds, he told all the stories he knew—

from Cinderella on. The soldiers began to take a liking to him and treated his wounds and eventually released him. We never know when we may need to be able to tell a story well.

BRINGING THE FAMILY TOGETHER

This book began with a brief statement about the way in which our society has developed a certain rootlessness over several generations. Fortunately, our society has turned its attention once more to the stabilizing influence of family and roots in preserving and developing some of the qualities that lead to fulfilled lives: a sense of belonging, enhanced communication, freedom for growth, and the need for support and encouragement.

Life story writing practiced "from within" can be one of the factors that leads to a more harmonious family life. Writing one's most vivid early memories brings many members of the family into the arena of one's life. Writing about significant characters gives unusual members of the family the opportunity to be seen and understood, for example, Uncle Eli and Ted Brown. Writing from several points of view allows family members to compare notes about important moments and to experience events each in his own way, knowing that most of us will disagree about both the facts and the meaning of any given circumstance. Pursuit of family history allows family members to glimpse stories from the past and the relationships out of which these stories have come. Additionally, this pursuit serves to help those who are shy know how important such revealing is to other members of the family. In sum, life story writing "from within" allows the many points of view within a family to be heard.

The actual process by which stories are exchanged may be a fascinating story as well. Distant families in which little sharing takes place can begin to dissolve some of the barriers. Closer families in which bonds are stronger may develop more of a sense of who each family member really is.

How the process has begun with one family is described with great charm in the story "Memories" by Judith Klein. Please see page 243.

LIFE STORY WRITING AND VALUES IN THE 21ST CENTURY

At the end of the twentieth century, the United States is an increasingly pluralistic and multicultural society. Our schools, legal, judicial, and welfare systems strain under the unfamiliar customs, habits, and language of those coming into our systems as well as the poor, homeless, and drug-damaged dwellers in our major cities.

What common ground do all of these people have? How can we as a society work toward common goals with such diversity around us? Seventy years ago the goal of every immigrant was to learn the language, customs, and habits of this country and to melt into American society while keeping some traditions alive.

This is not the goal of most immigrants today, nor of the poor and homeless. America's money, power, political freedom, and material opportunities are still desired. Its ideological and judicial elasticity are quite puzzling. Its humanistic concern for a highly developed, personal ability to grasp ideas and express them vigorously is little understood.

Storytelling is one thread which can weave all these diverse needs and desires together. The poorest and wealthiest touch one another through stories of struggle, humor, suffering, and compassion.

Storytelling cuts across all boundaries. Christian fundamentalist and existential humanist alike communicate through stories. Older adults touch the lives of children not through insistent and didactic moralizing but through stories of life's mysteries.

Every child in every classroom across the country can learn to tell and to share stories of his or her significant experiences in life. These stories are as precious to the child as a substantial bank account is to an adult. Each child needs to know how to put stories in and take stories out of his or her memory bank. For too long, story telling has been forgotten as a part of our educational system. From the lower grades through college, story telling through Life Story Writing will help build positive values and enhance self-esteem.

(For teachers who wish to employ some of what we have been exploring in this book, please see Appendix II for a format to follow. A forthcoming book, *Teaching Life Story Writing,* will explore this area in greater depth.)

Every segment of society profits by the ability to tell stories effectively. The homeless win refuge, abused children win safety, teachers win community support, and the disenfranchised win representation. Stories told well support each person's claim to truth and importance and win for each storyteller growing self-esteem. Plato tells us that everything we need to know already exists and our job is to penetrate through to our awareness of the truths that already lie within. One of the central questions asked by one of the popular human growth potential organizations is, "What is it that you know, that you are pretending not to know?" Parsifal, the great warrior-knight of the Grail Quest of the middle ages, is on this very path. His name (sometimes also spelled Perceval) means to pierce through or see through. His is the story of the warrior who sees through conventional definitions of what a warrior must be and discovers compassion in order to be reunited with his father. Family stories remind us of such values, conveyed in an entertaining way without insistence.

The stories of our personal past, even if we are tiny children, form the mythic path which we are to follow for the rest of our lives. Family stories lead to family traditions of compassion, dedication, self-sacrifice, and idealism. Family stories lead to family traditions of honest public service. Personal and family stories lead to citizens not molded by popular culture alone. A society in which personal and family stories are developed is a society in which survival values are strong.

I hope we will return storytelling to a place of honor within the family and in the classroom.

PART THREE

LIFE WRITING SELECTIONS

The stories that follow are selections from works written by students in life story writing classes in Los Angeles between 1983 and 1990. They were written using the techniques outlined in this book and serve as effective examples of the methods—and rewards—of writing from within. I hope you will find them enjoyable to read. They may stimulate in you recollections of a similar kind, recollections that you may someday want to write.

Selection One

Goin' South
by Rosalind Belcher

WHAT CAN BE MORE EXCITING THAN RIDING ON A Pennsylvania railroad train and you're seven years old and it's 1946?

"You're goin' home baby. Goin' home to Georgia. Goin' home to see yo' brothers and grandma and auntie."

That's what they told me.

Feeling grown up and scared at the same time. Opening up my boxed lunch of fried chicken, baloney sandwiches made with Wonder Bread and lots of mayonnaise, just like I like it. Eatin' all my lunch up, 'cept for my plums. Savin' them for dessert.

The train is movin' fast. I'm looking out the window. All the tall buildings are gone. Now I'm watching little box-like-looking houses that stand straight in a row. All the houses have three front steps leading to the doorway. Choo-choo choo-choo . . .

The nice tall man in the blue suit, wearing the funny hat that has a beak like a bird, walks up the aisle. His navy blue uniform has the shiniest gold buttons I've ever seen. They almost make me blink. He carries little pillows under his arms.

"Pillow? Pillow? Hi there little missy, would you like a pillow?"

He's talking to me. "Yes, I'd like a pillow."

"Here y'are missy; what's your name? Where ya going?"

"I'm going to Savannah," I answer, "I'm going to see my grandmother and auntie and brothers." I continue chewing the last bit of chicken in my mouth. Later, the man in the uniform smiles at me as he goes down the aisle giving the fat lady that just got on the train a little while ago a pillow. I never told him my name.

I hear him call out, "Baltimore, Baltimore!" He again moves up the aisle. He stops, not looking at me, "You, go back to that car, back there!" He never looked at me; his smile is all gone. I hate him. With my lunch box, pillow falling, even a hard boiled egg falls that I didn't know I had, I walk back. I hate him. Finally, I'm in the back of the train. All the faces back here are sad, tired, scared looking, faces of brown and black people.

Savannah, Georgia, 1946. I haven't seen my grandma or brothers or auntie since Mamma and I left with my other aunt three years ago. Mamma and I live up north now with Big Auntie. It still feels funny when I call Dot "Mother." One day, Big Auntie said, "Pumpkin, you should call your mother 'Mother,' and not Dot." "OK," I said. I've never called her Dot since. Seems just like it was yesterday they said, "Now it's time to go home and see the family. Make things better between all of us." That's why I'm on the train goin' to Georgia.

My brothers look really funny. Big, too. They talk funny. Say things like plait when they mean braid. Tote when they mean carry. It's fun. I'm talkin' like that too, in no time. Talkin' funny, havin' a ball.

One day, Big Mamma says to Auntie, who we call Sister, "Sister, take Pumpkin and the boys with you today when you deliver the ironin'. Stop by yer Cousin Suzy's house so she gets a chance to see Pumpkin. Let Pumpkin show off and talk proper-like." I'm feeling excited inside. I'm going to meet a new relative. Hot dog!

Me and the boys trail Sister down the dusty Georgia streets. Walkin' down West Broad Street, lookin' at the funny stores side by side; beauty parlor, barbershop, funeral parlor, market. Lookin' at the dusty boys shootin' their dusty marbles in the dusty streets while the little girls chase each other with dusty shoes and dusty legs. Some are even barefoot. West Broad Street, Georgia. Hot. Mosquitoes nipping my arms and legs before I can swat 'em away. Me and the other boys don't say much. Every now and then we steal a glance at each other. Walkin' along West Broad Street with Auntie Sister deliverin' ironin'.

The last house on the corner is Cousin Suzy's. How far have we walked? What a pretty house. Daisies on top of daisies on each side of the walkaway. Pretty white house, white shutters, pretty daisies. "Cousin Suzy," Sister calls, "Cousin Suzy, it's me, Sister and the churin'." From out of the screen door comes this little round lady with this red round face and even redder cheeks. Her brown hair is almost on her shoulders. Her eyes are green and they're smiling at me. She stops and says. "Hush yo' fuss gal, I hear ya. Come on 'round the back of the house. Hello there, you must be Pumpkin," she says to me. How can this white lady be our Cousin Suzy, I wonder, as a quiet hello comes out of my mouth. She gives us lemonade, and before we can finish she is sort of shooing us on our way. She gives Auntie Sister the $3.00 for the ironin' and says, "Give yer Ma my regards. Now you little ones better get goin' before it gets dark." It's a long time before dark.

It's nighttime now. I'm lying in my bed. The house is quiet. I've lived through another hot Georgia day. I hear Sister crying as she talks to Big Mamma in the room next door. She's telling Big Mamma how bad it makes her feel every time Cousin Suzy makes her come 'round the back of the house. I hear Big Mamma say, "Oh God, Sister, how can people be so hateful?" As I drift off to sleep, I see my friend in his uniform on the train giving out the pillows, then I see him makin' me go to the back of the train. I see Cousin Suzy makin' us go to the back of the house. A tear rolls down my face and I wonder, is this why me and Mamma left Georgia?

◊ ◊ ◊

Roz gives us a vivid picture of what it is like to be young, innocent, and black in the 1940s. Using colorful dialogue, an unintrusive narrative, and illuminating inner monologue, the writer enables us to feel what young Roz feels—how differently people behave toward her once the Mason-Dixon line has been crossed, only because she is black.

E S C A P E   T O   F R E E D O M
by Rose Saposnek

1. MY EARLY LIFE IN RUSSIA

BARDITCHEV WAS A CHARMING LITTLE FARM TOWN IN Russia of about two thousand farmers and their families. Jews and Christians lived peacefully side by side. Acres of wheat and corn fields skirted the town.

Main Street on Sunday was quite lively as the farmers and their families gathered to sell their wares and socialize. Dressed in my Sunday best, I waited with Mamma impatiently as Papa harnessed the family horse and hitched the horse to the wagon. We then drove to Main Street, where we were greeted warmly and socialized. Papa usually bought me a trinket and, best of all, he bought me some *saharni maroz* (ice cream).

Later in the afternoon we would ride far out in the country, passing farm after farm, passing Papa's old wooden one-room school house and the water hole farther down where Papa and his school friends swam. Sitting so high up on the wagon between my parents, I could see patches of watermelon and cantaloupes nestled in the fields.

But too soon trouble started and anti-Semitism reared its ugly head. Papa then decided to leave for America and would send for Mamma and me. The family was saddened but agreed that was the best plan.

I became more dear to my grandparents as they remarked how closely I resembled their son—my father. Grandpa was a tall and sinewy man, a hardworking and quiet person. He had sandy hair and blue eyes, eyes that had a twinkle only for me. I spent most of my time following him around the farm after Papa left. I remember my grandfather milking a cow. As I stood watching and listening to the squirting of the milk into the pail, I stuck my hands into the pail, feeling the warmth of the milk and washing my face with it. Grandpa laughed and gently scolded me.

Although the horses frightened me and kept me at a distance, I loved all the other animals on the farm. Once I was brave enough to cuddle a baby chick while the mother hen protested loudly.

Grandma was a no-nonsense and serious person. She was dark-complected, with brown, serious eyes. Although Grandma was only in her mid-forties, she was quite wrinkled. Housekeeping and cooking for seven of us kept her busy.

2. ESCAPE

The year 1917 in Odessa was very scary. People gathering in groups in the streets were exchanging stories of atrocities and killings that they heard were happening in nearby towns. I overheard Mamma talking to neighbors, asking each other where would they go, where would they hide if suddenly the Cossacks appeared.

I remember being awakened one morning by shooting and crying outside. I ran to the bedroom window and as I looked out, I could see soldiers with guns guarding our neighbor's house.

"Mamma, Mamma," I cried.

She came running, holding her hands to her chest.

"Look," I said, pointing to the window.

We stood terrified, watching the Cossacks in their gray uniforms and black caracul hats pulling out our neighbors, who were struggling and crying out in bewilderment. Their six children ranging from two to thirteen years of age, some of them my playmates, were also dragged along to the rear of the house, where they were all lined against the wall of the house and riddled with machine-gun fire—all eight of them.

Quickly we ran to a neighbor's house. There they led us down to the cellar, where families were sitting huddled together. A single candle was the only light. When guns sounded closer, Mamma decided to brave the way to her friend's house.

I remember holding tightly to Mamma's hand as we said our good-byes to the neighbors and hurried out of the cellar into the street. The streets, once so beautifully lined with lacy trees, with people bustling about through fashionable shops, couples holding hands and looking longingly into jewelry store windows at sparkling diamonds, were now in ruins. I saw charred trees, gaping store windows, crumbling buildings and dismembered bodies lying in full view.

We arrived breathlessly at the house where Mamma's friend lived, only to be stopped at the foot of the stairs by two young, sadistic looking soldiers.

"Halt," they commanded, one pointing a gun at us while the other demanded money. Mamma had sewn all of her savings in the back of her blouse. Picking me up with trembling hands and holding me tightly, she was thinking that if she were killed, I might as well be killed also.

"Hand over all of your money, Jew," the Cossack demanded. Mamma denied that she had money. He began to search her, almost reaching the back of her blouse, when the other soldier, becoming bored with the whole thing, put down his gun and said, "Ah, leave them go and find others."

Mamma weakly led me up the stairs to find all of the family slaughtered. As we heard someone walking up the stairs, Mamma quickly pulled me under a bloody blanket that covered a dead body. She smeared our faces and hair with blood.

"Hush," Mamma whispered.

Soon soldiers arrived.

"They are all dead," one said as he tapped Mamma with the butt of his gun to make sure. When we heard them leave, we then ran to a Christian friend of Mamma's. She not only offered us shelter, but also told us of a man that helped people like us cross the border to freedom. My mother took this chance.

◊

It was midnight as my mother woke me gently. As she dressed me, she told me in a hushed tone to be very quiet. It was dark and I was too sleepy to ask questions. Mamma picked me up and carried me quietly out into the darkness. We were going to steal across the Russian border. I must have fallen asleep again, for the next thing I remember we were waiting near a huge body of water—the Black Sea. The full moon outlined a man rowing a boat toward us. The lapping of the waves was the only sound in the silent night.

Mamma whispered to me. "This nice man," she pointed, "will row us across the sea. We must be very quiet," she cautioned again. As he helped us into the tiny boat, I took a dislike to the stranger. He smelled bad and he had a leering smile. No words were spoken as we got into the row boat. The boat rocked dangerously as he stepped in and sat down facing us. Picking up the oars, he smiled his leering smile at us. I could feel Mamma's body tense. It was cold and dark, the moon only reflected the blackness of the Black Sea. I buried my face with my hands so as not to see him.

"Hey, *malinka jevitsky* (little girl)," he sneered gleefully, sensing my distress, "if you make one move, the boat will tip over and we'll all drown in this black sea, ha, ha," he laughed wildly. The man was drunk. Mamma drew me closer to her as she quietly started to pray.

"Dear God," I heard her say, "please help me through this ordeal as you have helped me before, please for my child's sake." Mamma always talked to God, but it frightened me to see her cry.

"Please, Mamma," I pleaded, "don't cry."

Then like a miracle, the man changed.

"Don't worry, woman," he said gruffly, "I'll get you on land." He was quiet the rest of the trip.

It was still dark as we reached the shore. He helped us out of the boat. Mamma asked the man, "Where are we now?" He shrugged his shoulder and said, "You are in Rumania. There are farms nearby; the rest is up to you." He took his money and rowed away into the darkness. I began to cry. It was so cold and dark. Mamma firmly took my hand and pulled me along. It was getting lighter as we walked and soon we heard dogs barking. A farmer being alerted by his barking dogs was standing by his farm with a gun. We must have been a pitiful sight as we approached him. Without questioning us, he led us into the house, where his wife was preparing breakfast.

Once more Mamma's prayers were answered.

◊ ◊ ◊

In this story we see the author giving us a vivid picture of the events through sharp, spare detail and dialogue. What shines through so powerfully is the character of the mother whose quick, aggressive thinking at every turn is responsible for her own survival and that of her child.

FESSEX, FESSEX, PRENEZ GARDE!

by Isidore Ziferstein

THE TWO SAMMYS (MY COUSIN SAMMY YAGOLNITZER AND my schoolmate and friend Sam Rosenberg) and I are now at the age when we do a lot of girl-watching from a safe distance. We not only watch, we also drool.

But alas! not one of the girls we drool over even gives us a second look. We're convinced that the three of us are doomed to eternal bachelorhood. We talk a lot about this. We talk a lot about girls. After much deliberation, we arrive at the unanimous conclusion that all girls are by nature hard-hearted and cruel, that girls take a perverse pleasure in looking infinitely appealing, and then teasing and depriving the likes of us.

The only logical antidote to being forever lovesick and frustrated is: Strike back at the monsters! Show them our contempt! Show them that our hearts are pure; that we are above and beyond temptation by those wanton frails. We are, and shall always be, committed and sworn woman-haters.

The three of us form an exclusive, secret club, with a constitution and bylaws. The name of our threesome shall be "The Anti-Fessex League." (Fessex is our patented top-secret code-word for the fair sex.)

Our constitution begins with the immortal words of the Declaration of Independence: "When in the course of human events it becomes necessary for one gender to dissolve the bonds which have enslaved it to the other gender, and to assume the separate and equal station to which the Laws of Nature and of Nature's God entitle it . . . ." Our constitution then proceeds with appropriately modified excerpts from the Preamble to the Constitution of the United States, the Emancipation Proclamation, and Lincoln's Gettysburg Address, and ends with the ringing declaration that "We mutually pledge our Lives, our Fortunes, and our sacred Honor to the cause of freeing the males of this world from the yoke of enslavement by the so-called Fair Sex."

The bylaws require and pledge each of us, whenever and wheresoever we encounter a female of the opposite sex, to throw down the gauntlet, and challenge her with our battle-cry, "Fessex, Fessex, Prenez Garde!"

Not long after the formation of the Anti-Fessex League, I am invited by my friend Meyer Rosenbaum to his younger sister Bella's Sweet Sixteen party. I have been secretly in love with Bella for years. She looks adorable in her King Tut haircut—short, with its crescent curve, and points jutting out over her cheeks at the bottom of the crescent. For years I have hoped that Bella would reciprocate my deep abiding, though unspoken, true love. But she, cruel dame, knows nothing of my love. She goes out with older "men," who have steady jobs and coins jingling in their pockets. Just like a woman, she has chosen money over true love. I hate her for being so profligate and mercenary.

However, at the mere mention of Bella's name, my

heart melts. In flagrant violation of my vows to the Anti-Fessex League, I had written a long poem, in emulation of John Milton's "L'Allegro." It begins with the following verse:

> "Bella, oh beautiful Bella!
> Thy name doth thee not justice.
> For in heaven thou art called Bellissima."

And now I'll be a guest at Bella's party. Oh, joy! I accept Meyer's invitation a little too eagerly. My eagerness could betray my long-kept secret to Meyer. But Meyer doesn't notice. I ask Meyer airily,

"Is it OK if I bring a friend, a boy, that is, to the party?"

"Sure, it's OK," says Meyer, "Bella has invited all her girlfriends and she's worried that there won't be enough boys."

Too many girls?! Not enough boys?! Oh, glory! Ah, bliss! I'll invite my fellow woman-hater Sam Rosenberg to join me in sin.

Sam accepts my invitation to help fill the gender gap at Bella's party. But he says, "Izzy, I'm just doing this as a favor to you. I remain true to the cause of woman-hating, and I hope you will too."

The party is well-attended. Boys and girls overflow all the rooms of the Rosenbaum railroad flat. There are awkward introductions. The girls blush and giggle a lot.

These lovable, timid blushers and gigglers, are they the dangerous creatures against whom we have sworn a vendetta?!

The introductions are followed by dancing to the music of the Rosenbaum's brand new player-piano. I manage to get a dance with Bella. I am overjoyed. Bellissima is in my arms! I am so excited that my feet don't follow the rhythm of the player-piano music. I all but step all over Bella's feet.

After these preliminaries, we settle down to the serious business of the party—kissing games: "Spin the Bottle," "Post Office," "Wink," and more. I get to kiss almost all the girls. And I discover that I do not hate them at all. I love every one of them. They are so lovely, and tender, and so soft to the touch!

Carried away by all the dancing, and hugging, and kissing, I have all but forgotten about my friend, my comrade-in-arms and fellow woman-hater, Sam Rosenberg. The last time I saw him, he had been standing in a corner of the room glaring angrily at me and at the girls I was so ingloriously kissing. Why isn't Sam joining in the fun? Could it be because he is two years younger than I, and at fourteen he is not old enough to appreciate the ecstasy of kissing games?

Now Sam strides over to where I'm sitting in the circle of revellers, grabs my shoulder, and hisses, "Izzy, I wanna talk to you, right now!" I follow him obediently into the corridor. Sam is now shouting, "Izzy, I'm ashamed of you, and disgusted. How can you so degrade yourself! I'm leaving this house of ill-fame right now, and you're coming with me."

I'm torn between my loyalty to Sam and my new-found love for all sixteen-year-old girls in the world. Sam stalks out of the house. He expects me to be strong, and to follow him. But, alas, I am weak. I return to the festivities in the Rosenbaum's front room.

And so begins my fall from grace. No sooner am I confronted with the first temptation than, through weakness of character, combined with the power of the raging juices, I break the faith. I become helplessly and hopelessly bewitched by girlkind. I am a traitor to the cause of Anti-Fessex.

◊ ◊ ◊

In this story, Isidore has brought us into intimate touch with the experience of being sixteen. A psychi-

atrist, Isidore has made the transition from the abstract, jargon-ridden writing of his field into vivid, intimate personal writing. His story is told in the present tense, has plenty of dialogue, and tells us what he is thinking and feeling from one moment to the next. Isidore keeps to the spine of the story from the first moment to the last. As with so many humorous stories, the writer is not afraid to poke fun at himself. In the process, he reminds us how we were at that age, with our fears and our resolves. In fact, his story reminds me of a time when I was fourteen and ran away from the girls at a New Year's Eve party for fear of being kissed. Ah, youth.

THE *ANSCHLUSS* OF AUSTRIA
by Edith Ehrenreich

THE FIRST TWELVE YEARS OF MY LIFE I LIVE IN Vienna, the city where I was born. To me it seems the greatest and most beautiful city in the world. When I am about eight or ten years old, I invent a detective game. My friend and I play it whenever we have time. This is the way it works: We stand behind an apartment-house door and we count to ten. Then we step out onto the street, and the first person who passes us, we trail wherever they go. The game is to follow them without them noticing us. We spend hours following people from one end of the city to the other. Nobody ever notices us. Soon we know the city inside out. I love that game, because I love the old streets, the old houses. I like the atmosphere.

My parents and I live in a rather small and dingy apartment. Few people own their own house, or even a car, so the streets are filled with people walking, catching streetcars, shopping; the streets are busy with hustle and bustle.

I like the city; but I learn soon that I don't really belong—I am considered different.

One day in 1934, my mother and I are going through the inner part of the city, close to the Ring. Suddenly we hear shots nearby. People are running in all directions. No one seems to know what has happened. Later that day we find out that the Prime Minister has been assassinated. The government has now been taken over by the Christian Republicans.

The first thing they do that affects me is to introduce prayers in the schools. There are four Jewish children in my class of about thirty-five. We do not participate in the morning prayers. I realize that we are the objects of both envy and resentment. One schoolmate says to me, "How come you don't have to do this? Don't you believe in Christ?" Well, then the whole business of religion is dredged up, and soon some of our classmates call us Christ-killers and other fine names.

My friend Ilse and I are walking to school. We have been schoolmates since the first grade. Since September we have been in the fifth grade, attending a new private school for girls. It is April 1938.

We are going the same way as usual. It is a sunny April morning, kind of breezy. We walk pretty fast. We will get into trouble if we are late. Finally we come to this huge, heavy wooden door in a tall stone building. It is always hard to open this door. We come in, and we are surprised how quiet it is. Nobody is downstairs. Maybe we are late and classes have started. We look up the staircase, and on the second floor, along the banister, a lot of girls are standing. I recognize some of my classmates. They are looking at us. Under the banister is a big sign made of white butcher paper. In large capital letters the sign says: "PIGS AND JEWS ARE NOT ALLOWED TO ENTER HERE."

Then it becomes very noisy. Everybody is shouting and laughing and throwing stuff: erasers, crayons, notebooks, balled-up papers. It is like a birthday party in reverse. Ilse and I stand there for a while. It seems a long time. We look at each other. We run down the street. We slow down and cross an open area in an outdoor market. A man comes toward us. When he is about ten feet away from us, he says: "Jew dogs!" And then he spits.

Ilse and I continue walking. We come to the park by our house. We are very warm now and out of breath. We run to a bench. The bench has chalk writing on it: "For Aryans only." We look for a bench without any writing. Only one bench has a sign in red paint: "For filthy Jews only."

This was the day after the *anschluss* (annexation) of Austria to Germany. Ilse and I walk back to our own homes. We are scared. We know life will not be the same again.

My life changes considerably. I attend no school for a while, until a school for "Jews only" opens up. We are evicted from our apartment, and rent a room from another Jewish family, which is also in the process of being evicted. So we move from one family and one room to another. My father was employed in a synagogue. Now he has no job because the Temple was set on fire and burned down.

My father takes me to visit my grandfather in Czechoslovakia for the first time. I'm looking forward to the visit. He is the only grandparent I have who is still alive.

Grandfather lives in a small village. He meets us in front of his house in the courtyard. I expect a hug and a smile. Instead, he places his hand in front of my face and asks me to kiss it. I'm shocked. I never had to do this before. I don't like it.

During my few weeks stay at his house, there are a number of things he does that I really dislike. He corrects everything I do. I don't fold the tablecloth the right way; I don't know the prayers well enough; my manners need to improve. One day, when my step-grandmother prepares my most favorite dish, he takes a huge portion for himself, but doles out a most skinny little helping for me.

I find myself trying to stay out of his way. I am disappointed in him. I am glad to leave when my father comes to pick me up. I have no wish to visit him again. There is little love lost between us.

My father gets arrested. We think we will never get to see him again. By some miracle he gets released because of his Czech citizenship. We know it is only a matter of time now, and that next time we may not be saved. Every knock on the door makes our heartbeat stop.

And then, one day in August 1939, the long awaited permit to emigrate finally comes in the mail. It feels exactly like a reprieve from a death sentence.

In September, on the eve of Yom Kippur, our Day of Atonement, we are actually on the train that is going to lead us out of this hell. On this train are other Jewish people. I make friends with one of the girls my age. We travel throughout the night, but no one sleeps. The men say the prayers appropriate for the Holiday. There is such a feeling of hope and gratitude in all of us.

Morning time comes. We have finally come to the last station which is in the city of Cologne, the border town between Germany and Holland. Everyone gets off and turns in their passports to the Station Master for inspection. There are about 60 people all together. We drag off our belongings. My parents and I sit among the others, waiting to be called to board the shuttle train which will lead us into Holland. No one is eating. The Day of Atonement is a fast day. We don't even feel hungry. We just talk to each other in quiet voices.

Soon the names are called. One by one, each family boards the shuttle train that will take them across the

border to Holland. Our friends are called. We just wave
to them, knowing we'll see them soon on the train.
Pretty soon everyone's name has been called except
ours. To our horror, we see the train pulling away from
the station. My parents run over to the Station Master.
They can't believe that this is happening to us. He
shakes his head. We are not allowed to cross the border.
He says, "You are Czech citizens and Czechoslovakia is
considered an enemy country."

I look at my parents. There is no color in their
faces. They are standing speechless. A policeman, very
tall and well-built, comes to take us to the police station. Then we know that our death sentence has not
been commuted. My whole body starts to shake. My
father lifts the heavy trunks. My mother and I carry a
smaller suitcase, but it feels as if it contains lead. We
walk a long distance through the city streets. My father
stops every once in a while to catch his breath. The
sweat is pouring down his face. My mother tries to pick
up the trunks and wants to carry them a few steps, but
my father grabs them away from her. The policeman
keeps prodding him along. People stare at us. I hear
them saying, "Look at the Jews!" I hold my head as
high as I can. I don't look at anyone.

After a long time we arrive at the police station.
We are told to sit and wait until the police chief comes.
We sit on a wooden bench. I sit next to my father. My
mother is on the other side of him. I cannot see her
face. I don't want to look at her.

It is a well-lit, roomy place. It is Sunday morning.
We are told that the police chief is not at the station
yet. We sit in absolute silence. I look only at the door. I
keep thinking: "We should run away as fast as we can.
Why are we sitting here?" I look at my father's face for
a moment. I see tears running down. I have never seen
my father cry before. I feel like vomiting.

Occasionally the phone rings. There are no other

sounds in the place. I don't know how long we sit there. A policeman finally comes out of the office. We have not seen him before. He tells us that the police chief is still at home, but that he will call him to find out what to do with us. Now we all know: the answer means life or death. I keep thinking, "We have no power at all. It all depends on one man who doesn't even know us, whether we live or die. Why should anyone have this right?"

Then the door to the office opens again. I don't look up. I am not breathing. The policeman says to my father: "The police chief said to let the Jews go." We stand up. My father puts his arms around me and my mother. He is sobbing. I think, "If I were God I would destroy the whole country this moment."

After our reprieve from the police chief, I hardly remember our way back to the train station. But we carry all our stuff back. It seems a lot lighter. A shuttle train is provided for us, and we are the only passengers on board. It is about a five minute ride across the border. It is early afternoon. The sun is shining directly through the train window. It is bright.

Soon we are at the train depot in Holland. We have not slept for thirty-six hours, we have not eaten or taken a sip of liquid for an equal amount of time, and we have just experienced one of the most traumatic events of our lives. The sweat is still pouring from us; our tear-stained faces and our wrinkled clothes are a sight to behold.

The Dutch train looks more like the inside of a streetcar. All seats are occupied.

As soon as my parents and I get on, three or four people jump up from the bench facing the door. I am sure that they can't stand the sight of us and want to get away. But, no! They grab our belongings and stack them in the overhead luggage compartment. Then they come toward us and ask us to take their seats. My father, who never wants to accept anything from anybody, shakes his head. But they take him firmly by the arm and seat him on the bench. Someone, I can't remember who, gently leads me to a seat next to my parents. One lady, who speaks excellent German, asks us if we are refugees. All we say is, "Yes!" Within minutes half a dozen people come over to us and bring us all kinds of food. Coffee and bread with cheese for my parents. I get hot chocolate, a box of candy, and an apple. We sit there in absolute astonishment. For about a year and a half we have been in constant fear of our neighbors, even our so-called friends. And now these perfect strangers treat us as if we were their long-lost family.

When we arrive in Rotterdam, one of the Dutch people calls the Jewish Agency for us and waits with us until we are picked up and taken care of.

We stay for six weeks in Holland until we are able to board the ship which brings us to America. Those are the best weeks of my youth. To this day, whenever someone tells me that they are Dutch, I feel related to them.

I never saw my grandfather again. He was exterminated along with millions of other European Jews before I had a chance to forgive him for his petty idiosyncrasies, and ask his forgiveness for my own lack of love and respect. To this day, whenever I think of him, I feel a deep sense of guilt.

◊ ◊ ◊

Edith's story has a strong shape to it. Innocent freedom in the beginning, then humiliation, the struggle to survive, hope, a hint of tragic inevitability, and finally freedom and belonging. Edith tells the story in the present tense and provides us with a mosaic of details which give us a sense that we are actually in the experience.

SELECTION FIVE

UNCLE ELI
by Rose Rothenberg

UNCLE ELI WAS A CHARACTER. HE WAS MY FATHER'S oldest brother and the second son in a family of six whose members differed from one another in many ways. But Eli was really different. For one thing, he was a bachelor. When I was a little girl of six or seven and Uncle Eli was in his mid-forties, his single state was already accepted by the family as not very likely to change.

True, there was a story circulating about how close to matrimony he had once come. With his slim, straight carriage, wavy brown hair, expressive eyes and regular features, he certainly was not unattractive. In fact, in his mid-thirties he was considered quite a catch. To the young widow, Ruth, he seemed quite a likely prospect. The death of her ailing first husband had released Ruth from years of dutiful attendance upon him. Now, staring into the third decade of her life, she turned her energy and attention to finding a new husband. The introductions had come about through a remote relative who certainly must have known my uncle only superficially. Though he had never looked upon marriage with favor, Uncle Eli was smitten with Ruth. She was fair to look upon and one could not ask for a more refined and cultured lady. Uncle Eli noted with satisfaction, also, that she was gainfully employed as a milliner.

He pressed the courtship with ardor and in short order they were engaged. They discussed wedding plans with pleasure and care. They agreed upon their future living arrangements. Things were hopping along quite smoothly. It was the honeymoon discussion that brought the courtship to a grinding halt. You see, the bride-to-be dearly wanted to honeymoon in nearby Atlantic City, which in the twenties was the place to go. Uncle Eli balked. It was one thing to get married but quite another to incur such an unnecessary expense.

Not that he couldn't afford it. My father and uncle had both labored hard at their trade as metalsmiths. But while my father was weighed down with wife and kids and had not a penny in the bank, Uncle Eli had already amassed a small fortune.

You may well question that a metalsmith, even an unmarried one, could have acquired a sizable nest egg so early in life. I assure you it was perfectly possible if you lived as my uncle did. He was a boarder and had his room on the third floor rear in a neighborhood that had seen better days in the past—the very distant past. After a time he figured that he was paying too much for board. He was a delicate eater and could hardly do justice to the hearty meals served by the "missus." He became instead a steady customer at the local kosher restaurant. Here he could order and pay for just what he could eat. Moreover, it became clear that if he started his day a little later he could easily make do with two meals rather than three. The arrangement proved so satisfactory that he continued in this way for thirty-some years, at which time the restaurant went out of business.

Uncle Eli was a dapper man and extremely meticulous about his person. His shirts were always pure white, at least until they yellowed a bit with age. His dark serge suit was always well pressed and clean. It did not yellow with the passage of time, but took on a shine that competed with the gloss he maintained on his high-button shoes. In the summer months he sported spotless white buckskin oxfords—the same pair year after year. His straw hat was worn at a rakish angle and, rain or shine, he was never without an umbrella.

Uncle Eli felt no great need for entertainment or divertissement, though he did indulge at times and pay the ten cent admission to a movie. Occasionally, too, he walked the few miles into town and climbed to the topmost gallery to attend a matinee concert at the Academy of Music.

So, you see, it was impossible for Uncle Eli not to have acquired some money. Atlantic City was certainly not out of reach financially. It simply made no sense to him to spend money on a honeymoon. Nevertheless, he was not an unreasonable man; Ruth was very desirable and he was more than willing to compromise. He told his lady love that they would marry and that he would bankroll *her* visit to Atlantic City for a few days and *he* would remain behind in Philadelphia and wait for her. Upon such stunning revelation of what life with my uncle would be, Ruth's dream of marriage and security exploded. She broke the engagement forthwith.

Well, so much for romance. Anyhow, it certainly must have soured Uncle Eli on marriage because he remained a lifetime bachelor.

Uncle Eli was sociable to a degree. He visited our house often but never stayed very long. Now, our house was just as clean as any other that had half a dozen kids dashing about. Even so, when Uncle Eli put in an appearance my mother quickly surveyed the parlor and removed any appearance of dirt. But Uncle Eli, before seating himself, extricated his white handkerchief and with a few swift flourishes dusted the chair that was offered him. Only then did he carefully lower himself to the edge of the chair, hook his umbrella on his arm, remove his hat and with the cuff of his jacket give it a quick swipe and place it on his knee. He was ready to visit.

My parents raised us to respect our elders, and asking visiting relatives for anything was certainly frowned upon. In the case of my uncle there was an exception. If it happened that he visited on a warm summer evening, my father might hint broadly that it would be nice for the children to have an ice cream treat. That was our signal to begin pleading with my uncle for money. Uncle Eli would sit like a block of wood while my father laughingly encouraged our efforts. Sometimes our wheedling paid off and my uncle doled out three cents each for a single-dip cone. Having succeeded this far, we usually explained that just a penny more would get us a sprinkling of chocolate jimmies over the ice cream. But he would protest that we wanted the moon and would shoo us from his presence. We considered it a victory anyway because we recognized that Uncle Eli had limits.

The years were not kind to Uncle Eli. He lost a good bit of his hearing and he became even more reclusive. My father and he could communicate during his infrequent visits only because my father was blessed with sturdy lungs and the will to use them. My mother, after a few attempts at polite conversation, would escape to the kitchen with her hands over her ears. By this time we children had outgrown the game of trying to pry money from Uncle Eli and he generally ignored us.

As the years piled up, my uncle's eccentricities became a matter of great concern to my father and his sisters. Eccentric behavior had deteriorated into plain craziness. His earlier attention to cleanliness of person gave way to complete indifference about his attire. It became ever more apparent that the shirts were not being laundered regularly, and the suit had long outlived its respectability. The shoes, dull and scuffed, needed to be reheeled. The handkerchief that was still whipped out to dust a chair had done duty too long. He had long since been persuaded to turn over his financial affairs to a nephew by marriage whom he trusted, and he was never in want. Nevertheless, it took the combined efforts of my father and his sisters to convince him from time to time to buy a new wardrobe.

Uncle Eli was well into his eighties when he was finally prevailed upon to turn over his remaining assets to the Jewish Home for the Aged in return for lifetime care. Death claimed him there at age 93.

I often think about the strange life my uncle lived and wonder what story I would now be telling had he embarked on that honeymoon trip so long ago.

◊ ◊ ◊

The story takes us through several of the more revealing moments of Uncle Eli's life. The writer gives us a clear view of his fastidious, even miserly ways. Rose accomplishes this despite the fact that the story contains no dialogue and no inner monologue. The details of expression and action, even the background of his engagement to Ruth, give us a very clear picture of his life. Nevertheless, a little more dialogue might make this wonderful picture even more vivid. I would love to hear the kinds of things Uncle Eli said.

SELECTION SIX

THE TYPHOON OF FORTY-FIVE

by Edward R. Boyle

FINAL VERSION

A S A YOUNG SAILOR IN 1945, I SERVED AS A SIGNALMAN
aboard a patrol craft. They were the smallest real
fighting ships in the navy. These ships were only 120
feet above the waterline. The mast rose 35 feet above
the deck and the yardarms stretched out to ten feet.
She carried a wartime crew of 125 men. On her bow
was mounted one five-inch gun which could exchange
fire with any surfaced submarine. On her main deck,
fore and aft of the bridge and wheelhouse, were 20mm
anti-aircraft guns, four on each side. Our stern was
decorated with two twin 40mm pom-pom anti-aircraft
guns. We had plenty of firepower if we got into a big
scrap. The one gun we had on the flying bridge was at
my battle station, a .50 caliber machine gun, jokingly
called "Boyle's Pea Shooter." I only mention this gun
because I was not allowed to shoot it. The captain
grinned when he assigned me this station. "I want you

on the bridge, Boyle, but don't fire that damn gun. You'll wipe out half our crew." I might have, too.

The smallness, speed and maneuverability of our patrol craft made her a rather hard target to hit. Our larger fighting ships often thought we were pests until we got into a scrap and started biting. Then they were glad to have us on their side.

Our assigned station was three miles outside the harbor of Okinawa, a stretch of ocean six miles long. In this stretch of ocean we patrolled back and forth, using our sonar to detect enemy submarines and our radar for spotting aircraft. Every man on deck and on the bridge was trained as a lookout, no matter what his other duties were.

The day the typhoon hit was like so many other days at sea. The sun rose in the east, the sky was clear with a light breeze blowing, the ocean was like a sheet of fun-house glass. Just smooth lazy swells. At eleven in the morning we received a radio message that there were storms brewing southwest of our position. The captain ordered a close radio watch and double look-outs. He ordered them to keep an eye out for clouds and any change in the ocean that might occur.

Most of us were young men and had been through storms at sea before, so we gave it little thought. The sun was just as bright as ever and the sea had not changed since early morning. Still rolling gently were the soft swells that can lull you to sleep when at sea. The air was as fresh as an autumn day in the north woods. We could smell the faintest tinge of salt.

My regular watch was 12 noon to 4 P.M. I arrived on the bridge at 11:45. The signal man on duty, Stew Gray, informed me of the radio message. Laughingly he said, "Do you believe that, Boyle?" Then gazing at the horizon he added, "This is the nicest day we've had in a month." From our bridge we could see the horizon about 20 miles away, due to the curvature of the earth.

"Three hundred and sixty degrees, not a cloud in the sky, not even a ripple on the ocean. Nothing for us to worry about today," I answered. I relieved Stew of the duty and took charge of the bridge.

I placed the telescope in its stand and turned toward the harbor. Nothing seemed amiss there. The transports were all in their assigned places, and the cargo carriers were coughing up their insides to the many small boats that surrounded them like so many young birds being fed by their mothers. On the beach the small boats were unloading as quickly as possible and running back to their mother ships for another helping of whatever was being served. The supplies on the beach were being moved about, trucks running back and forth like armies of worker ants. This was like any other day of military operation, business as usual.

All was serene the first hour of my watch. Many off-duty men were sitting around on the deck enjoying the beautiful day. Those on duty went about their tasks maintaining the equipment they might have to use in case of a fight.

The sea began to get a little more restless, the swells a little larger, we could see a few whitecaps but still no clouds.

On the bridge were the captain, two lookouts, the boatswain's mate, always referred to as "Boats," and I. The captain, sensing trouble, ordered all watertight hatches closed. All equipment that might shift was tied down tightly. All hands who weren't really needed on deck were ordered below to their quarters.

I had overheard the captain requesting the officer of the deck to stay in the wheelhouse. He requested the O.D. [officer of the day] to monitor the course and speed orders that he would be giving from the bridge.

The captain then ordered those of us on deck into our foul-weather gear. I thought to myself, what the hell's the matter with him, until I noticed he was already in his gear.

One lookout was sent into the crow's nest 25 feet up the mast, where a lookout can stand with just his head sticking out and his view is increased by about five miles. The other lookout was sent to the stern lookout post. All lookouts were in communication with the bridge by telephone.

The boatswain was all over the deck, checking the waterproof muzzle covers on all the guns, seeing that the swivels were all locked properly so none of them would start swinging as the ship started to pitch and roll, setting up lifelines from bow to stern and to the ladders where anyone on deck might have to go.

I checked the equipment on the bridge. The flag bag was covered with its waterproof cover. I checked to be sure it would not blow off in a wind. I made sure the binoculars were clean and ready for use. There was very little on the flying bridge that could trouble us. Our lights were working properly. Everything was in order. It appeared we were having a big drill of some kind and I had just gotten stuck on the bridge.

It wasn't long after these precautions had been taken that the crow's nest shouted into the phone, "Rainclouds to the southwest, ten to fifteen miles." We could detect fear in his voice. All eyes immediately turned in that direction. I heard the captain gasp as if in silent prayer, "Oh, my God, I don't believe it." From southeast to northwest and as high as we could see into the sky was the most terrifying sight. Night was descending upon us and with it fearful lightning and even from this distance the violent crashing of thunder. Each stroke of thunder sounded like an explosion. When the lightning flashed it was as if the heavens were being torn apart. I waited for a voice to say, "Boyle, your time has come!"

Immediately the captain issued his first order.

"Get your ass the hell out of the crow's nest before you get it blown out! Take the forward post." To the wheelhouse, he shouted, "Pass the word to the engine room and the crew's quarters to hang on! We're going to be hit by something, just don't ask me what."

Being pushed ahead of this devastating sight was a wall of howling wind that screeched like a herd of banshees, and rain that felt like knives trying to cut the flesh from the bone.

From the wheelhouse came the O.D.'s voice, "The radar is out and we can't get a damn thing on sonar."

"Shut 'em down. They won't do us a hell of a lot of good in this weather anyway. Put two men on the wheel, you're going to need all the muscle you can get." That's all the captain could say before we were engulfed in a most awe-inspiring and terrific spectacle. Our world was thrown into convulsions. Sheets of water were climbing over the flying bridge. Every time we hit a swell our main deck was under water. The lookouts yelled, "We're lashing ourselves down to keep from being washed overboard." The lightning flashed so close I was sure I could reach out and touch it. I was sure it would destroy us. Close on the heels of the lightning came thunder. Not with a crash but with an explosion that lifted our ship right out of the water like a trout on a fly line, shuddering and shaking before dropping back into the water. I could hear the steel plates of the ship's hull strain as they were twisted to their limits. We were being bounced like a cork upon the raging sea. Each time the lightning flashed, it struck fear into our hearts. Its brightness so illuminated the sky that we thought the end of the world was upon us. The thunder was so deafening that no one on the bridge talked. We were at the mercy of the storm.

The initial fear did not last long. There was too much to do and it had to be done now. The captain was giving the wheelhouse instructions as to course and speed. Boats and I had one arm wrapped around the light standard, trying to keep our balance. Boats quipped, "Nice knowing you, Boyle. If we make it, I'll buy you one."

I hollered across the ten-foot space that separated us, "As long as we're still afloat we still have a chance." I wouldn't have bet my next check on it, though!

"Hey, Boats, where in hell's the flare gun?" bellowed the captain between cracks of thunder.

"It's in the small arms locker, sir."

The captain hesitated just a few moments. "We're going to need that gun on the bridge."

Now I was worried. The flare gun is used only if there is some grave emergency aboard ship, emergencies where the crew is in danger and may need to be rescued. I scrunched down into my foul-weather gear, hoping the captain couldn't see me. The next order I heard was, "Hey, Boyle, get that flare gun." I knew all along I would have to get it.

The big ships such as transports and cargo ships have passageways that a man can stand up in. Not our patrol craft, however. We were built the same as the larger ships, but were one-tenth the size. A sailor learns early in his career to stoop. No matter what door he goes through, he has to stoop or bump his head. I had to descend the flying bridge down to the wheelhouse and then down to the 'scope-room. Then I went through several three-foot-high passageways in total darkness before I could get to the gun locker and return. My work was cut out for me.

The captain ordered the ship turned so I could get into the wheelhouse without swamping it. I pounded the door. It was yanked open, and I was pulled inside. The door was slapped shut.

"What's going on topside?" all of the men wanted to know.

"We're catching hell from some kind of a storm," I answered. "The wind is blowing the rain straight at us, and the lightning and thunder scare the hell out of us." The flying bridge was better than being in the stuffy wheelhouse. The strain on the face of the men on the wheel showed. It took all of their concentration to keep the ship on course. I ripped off my foul-weather gear and piled it in a corner.

I told the O.D. where I was going and asked him, "Sir, if I'm not back in half an hour will you send someone after me?"

He laughed a little and answered, "Don't worry, Boyle, we won't leave you stuck anywhere."

In a far corner of the wheelhouse was a hatch two and a half feet wide. This led to the 'scope room. "Wish me luck, fellows, here goes nothing," I joked as I quickly opened the hatch and shimmied down to the 'scope room deck. One of the crew slammed the hatch before I had finished talking. The dim light from one red overhead bulb cast an eerie light about the eight-foot 'scope room. Even in these close quarters I had to hang on. The ship was still tossing and rolling wildly. I could imagine what was going on outside. I could hear the thunder crashing. I felt like I was inside a steel drum with someone beating on it.

From this compartment it was necessary for me to crawl through another horizontal tube to the engine room, a tube ten feet long and three feet high with only room to crawl on all fours. After entering I still had to shut the door behind me. This tube had no lights. Closing it was like sealing my own tomb. What I had to do now was to crawl straight ahead in the darkness until I hit my head. Opening the hatch, the engine room crew looked at me as if I were a ghost.

The chief bellowed, "What in hell are you doing down here?" And in the next breath, with a little more urgency, "What's going on topside?" Again I saw a look of grave concern among the men in the engine room. They put up with engine noise and oily-smelling heat all of the time they were standing watch. In rough weather, it was a hell-hole.

"All hell's breaking loose out there. When the lightning flashes and the thunder crashes it feels like we're being torn apart," I told them.

"Thanks, it feels like that down here, too," replied the chief. "We're getting some damn strange orders down here I'm glad we know what's happening." The engine crew looked a little shaky, but were very busy and had to stay alert. I had one more tube to go through to reach the crew's quarters.

One of the men hollered over the noise of the engine, "I'll hold the hatch open until you reach the other end. That way you won't hit your head so hard." I scooted through the tube in record time, bounced into the crew's quarters, and looked around. All of the men were at least stripped to the waist. Some were walking around in their shorts and some were in their bunks, too sick to move. The heat and the humidity and the smell of sweating bodies was stifling.

On the deck there were several inches of water sloshing back and forth. The water did its little dance on the deck every time the ship would pitch or roll. I glanced into the head. Some of the men had made it to the trough and were being sick. Some of them didn't make it that far. The deck was covered with a layer of stinking colored water which was sloshing around the head. The men who were sick didn't even care. I decided to stay on the bridge if I ever got back there. The noise of the storm was deafening in the crew's quarters. Every time a crash of thunder hit, it sounded like a sledgehammer being driven against the hull. Inside the ship the sound of twisting steel and the popping of rivets was magnified a hundredfold. I had my arms around the mast when an especially loud crash of thunder hit. As the ship rolled to port, I felt the mast twisting in my arms. I became so frightened that I quickly headed for the gun locker, grabbed the flare gun and ammunition and reversed course.

Going through the crew's quarters I told my watch relief, "Lee, you don't have to relieve me on the bridge. I'm wet already; no use you getting wet, too." I didn't tell him I was afraid to stay below. He didn't feel well and thought I was doing him a favor, so he agreed. I was happy to be heading back to the bridge and made record time getting there.

"How are things going below?" the O.D. asked, when I popped through the hatch. When I explained the conditions in the crew's quarters, he said, "Those poor devils. There's going to be a lot more of them sick before this thing is over." I hurriedly got into my foul-weather gear again and climbed up to the flying bridge.

Before the captain could say anything, I spoke up. "Captain, I'm all wet already, Lee is sick and he's willing to let me take his watch. Is it all right with you, sir?"

He smiled and answered, "I'm staying up here for the duration of the storm; if you want to keep me company it's all right with me." I sometimes wonder if he was scared too.

We were still patrolling our assigned area, trying to keep as close to the six-mile stretch as we could under these crazy conditions. We were pitching and rolling; water was still splashing over the flying bridge. Every time a flash of lightning exploded, I squinted my eyes.

The loudspeaker was hooked up on the bridge so we could hear radio messages from the other ships. Even if we felt alone, we knew by the messages being sent that other ships were having more trouble than we were. One in trouble was a sub-chaser, which was even smaller than the patrol craft. This ship not only had most of its electrical equipment knocked out, they also had engine trouble and could only produce ten knots speed. They were taking on water and if their pumps stopped they would have to abandon ship. The code books and all the messages had been put into a weighted bag to be thrown over the side if they had to abandon ship.

Boats and I had our searchlights working the water in front of us. There was a great deal of floating debris that either had washed off the ship's deck or had broken away from its mooring. We tried to steer clear of the debris.

Little note of time was made by the men on the bridge. It had been midnight since one in the afternoon. We finally received a message that lifted our spirits. All ships on picket duty were to return to the harbor and find mooring for the duration of the storm. Immediately, the captain ordered our navigator to the wheelhouse.

It was only moments later that we heard through the voice tube, "Lt. McDermott reporting, sir." And with a lilt of laughter, he added, "Want me to take you kids home?" The captain let out a hearty laugh. He knew we were on our way to a safe mooring place.

The captain told McDermott, "I'm going to give some course and speed orders from the flying bridge because of all the crap that's floating around."

McDermott answered, "I'll head you in the general direction and when we hit the harbor lights she's all yours."

We couldn't just turn the ship and head for the harbor. We would have the storm at our back and lose all control of the steering. We had to zig-zag as slowly as we could and still keep the ship under control.

Our searchlights were picking out quite an array of floating debris in the water now. One of the more dangerous objects was a floating dry dock. When Boats first spotted it with his light, he thought it was another ship. This dock bearing down on us looked like a three-story building ready to shove us out of the way. The captain changed course in a hurry. We passed within thirty feet of it. "That was too close for comfort. I'm goddamn glad we spotted it in time," sighed Boats.

After picking our way through tons of floating junk, we spotted a harbor light. The captain called down the voice tube, "We got a light, Mac. Come up long enough to identify." That's how long Mac stayed on the flying bridge. He had come up without his foul-weather gear, so within minutes he was soaked. But he did determine for us that the light we spotted was the east light. He then set our course to enter the harbor. The captain slapped Mac on his wet back, "Thanks, Mac. Get into some dry clothes. We'll take it from here."

We were able to find the harbor channel without any trouble. Getting through the channel was like plowing through a batch of bread dough. It seemed like all the water in the harbor was trying to get out at once. It felt like we would move ahead 20 feet and get pushed back 15. The swells from the harbor were as bad as those on the open sea. We passed the natural break-water. The thunder and lightning were as bad as on the open sea, and the rain still beat on us as if it were trying to drive us out of the area. Our job now was to find something to tie up to. When the lightning flashed, we could see many of the larger ships swinging on their anchor chains tugging to get loose. We could not tie up to any large ship, for if we did we would be crushed if it started to roll. We needed to find something closer to our size.

Like picket duty, we steamed back and forth, only in a much shorter path. The thunder was still deafening, but here the lightning was a blessing. Every flash lit up the harbor so we could see what we were up against. A brilliant flash silhouetted an anchor buoy about a quarter mile away. We steered for it. These anchor buoys are placed in harbors away from the docks and the shore, so large ships can tie up to them and be unloaded. They are about 20 feet across and made up of hollow drums banded together, with concrete poured over to make a solid deck. Anchored to the bottom of the harbor, they have a large ring in the center for the ships' lines.

The captain explained, "Boats, I'm going to pass close enough for you to jump and grab the ring."

Boats answered without hesitation, "Yes sir!"

We were all a little nervous. Boats took up his position outside the deck rail. The lookouts were in position with the lines ready to go and I was on the light. The captain made his approach, scraping some paint as he hit it. Boats made a nice four-point landing, catching the ring. We went past the buoy about 50 yards and had to back up to throw the lines. They went in a perfect arc and he had them tied down quickly. We all heaved a sigh of relief.

We were now snuggled up to a safe mooring and Boats could climb over the rail onto the deck. The captain hollered, "That was a hell of a nice piece of work, Boats. Well done."

The lightning flashed and the thunder crashed, but being safely moored, the storm no longer seemed so threatening.

The captain told the four of us to report to his cabin. He looked pretty well tired out when we entered. He smiled, "You men did one hell of a job." Handing each of us a half pint of medical brandy, he said, "You men have been topside for 20 hours. Drink this and stay in your sacks until you wake up." Then with a big grin on his face, he said, "Thanks, fellows."

◊ ◊ ◊

Ed's first draft of this story of a young man's initiation into the perils of the sea (see page 68) kept us at arm's length. The narrative was sketchy, the characters hazy. However, the final draft, using colorful dialogue and well observed detail and action, brings us right into the experience of moving through the bowels of the ship while the storm tosses it around like a cork. By bringing the protagonist's struggle into focus, the writer enables us to see what the story truly is: a seafarer's perilous struggle for survival as he descends into "hell" and returns.

MOM
by Louis Doshay

WHY DO I HAVE SUCH A HARD TIME WRITING ABOUT you? After all, you've been gone for thirty-four years now. So why does it still bring tears to my eyes? Maybe if I just imagine that I'm really talking to you, maybe then I can put it all down. Maybe then I can get the words out. And who knows? Maybe you can really hear me.

So why the tears? Is it because I still haven't let go? Yes, that might be part of it. You left us too soon. You died. Why do I have such a hard time saying that word? I guess it's too final, and I'm not done with you yet. And I never had time to do those things for you that I promised. I know you told me that I never would, but that just makes it hurt all the more. You were right when you said I would find a wife to do things for and give things to. But you were wrong when you said that then I would forget you.

And it hurts me that you never got the real joy that you deserved. You never saw two of your grand-children, David and Denise. Everyone says that Denise looks a lot like you did at her age. She's as beautiful as her sister, Doreen, but she has a *zoftik* figure, more like yours, and she has your round face. And you should see how tall David has grown. I'm four inches taller than Pop was, and David is four inches taller than I am. He is almost six feet tall.

But I ramble on about this and that, and I still don't talk about us. Surely our unfinished business has more to do with you and me. Remember when we were moving to California? I was fifteen then, and I was the navigator. I plotted our progress on the maps the Auto Club had given us, and gave Pop the directions for each change of highway. I can't remember what it was about, but you hit me. I got very angry at that, and I got out of the car and ran away. I was too proud to come back, but I didn't really want to get lost. So I walked down the side of the main highway toward Los Angeles. In about half an hour Pop found me, and I let him persuade me to get into the car. Pop was good at letting me get off the hook without my having to lose face.

That reminds me of that other time I ran away. I think I was about eight years old. Pop, you, and I were walking in Cratona Park after supper. I'm not really sure why you hit me that time either, but I suppose I could have been bugging you to buy me a penny's worth of "Polly" seeds from one of those walking salesboys who were always selling things in the park on summer evenings. I really was a stubborn kid, and I never gave up easily. When you hit me, I ran away and shouted I was never coming home again. Pop chased me for a little while, but he didn't have a chance of catching me. He was in his forties, and a little on the heavy side. I went to the other side of the park, near Fulton Avenue, and I sat down and felt sorry for myself. And I cried. You sent my brother, Manny, to find me. By the time he did, it was well after dark. Manny didn't waste time being diplomatic. He grabbed me by the scruff of the neck and took me home.

But those incidents are not the ones that bothered me the most. There were others that really hurt. Like when I was in the fourth grade, and I brought home my report card. I had one B and the rest all As. You told me, "So what good is that. Your brother, Carl, got straight As when he was your age. And what good did it do? He still quit college to marry that girl. And you'll do the same thing. You'll meet a girl, and you'll quit school and get married."

"No, I won't," I shouted. "You'll see. I'll finish college. You'll see." Well, you saw that I was right, and you were only two-thirds right. Oh, I met Sylvia and got married all right, but I didn't quit school until after I graduated. I didn't even quit when Doreen was born over a year before my graduation. I didn't even consider quitting, and Sylvia never suggested it. Not even the time when all we had in the house to eat for three days was pancakes and beans. Yes, what you had said made me determined to prove you wrong, but what a price I paid inside when I was little for that determination.

But I don't blame you any longer for that. I know that you gave me determination the best way you knew. Yet I still have to tell you that it hurt. I made sure I didn't made that mistake with my children, but I made my share of other mistakes.

And why don't I remember you giving me a hug? I don't remember hugging you. Those two things still hurt.

I remember the last time Sylvia, little Doreen and I came to see you before you died. Your hair was completely white in front and around the sides, even though you were only fifty-six. It framed your face beautifully, and I told you how great you looked. How were we to know you were right when you said you would die soon?

I love you.

◊ ◊ ◊

The death of his mother is the catalyst for Louis'
exploration of his inner feelings toward her: his sad-
ness, his anger, his resentment, his acknowledgment of
her point of view, and finally his forgiveness. Each mo-
ment of their past together is a tiny but very complete
vignette remembered with the sharpness and vividness
of a memory etched in pain.

Selection Eight

The Ad
by Inge Trevor

I COME HOME FROM WORK TIRED. IT IS A THURSDAY night toward the end of January. I open the mail box. There is an envelope from *New York Magazine*.

This is the thirtieth letter I have received since I placed an ad in the personal section. My late husband has been dead for two years and I am ready for a change.

My friends Rita and Jules convinced me to put the ad in the magazine. Me, a nice Jewish lady from Syracuse. Well, it worked for them, I think. But I'm beginning to get discouraged. Almost all the men I have met have been dogs.

I open the letter. It reads: "Dear Vivacious, Slender and Attractive: If you know the difference between sushi and *truite au bleu* or Hammarskjold and Hammerfest, please call 473-0608. A well-traveled, sophisticated European man will answer all your questions. Don."

This is a great letter. I like the writing too. Of course I know what sushi is. *Truite au bleu,* blue poached trout, I always ate in Switzerland. I know who Dag Hammarskjold is. Hammerfest is a town I believe, but where? I call my friend Renate. "It's in Norway," says my all-knowing girlfriend.

Reassured, I dial the number he gave me. "Hello," a friendly voice answers.

"I received your letter today," I reply.

"What is your name?" he asks. There is a slight foreign accent.

"Inge."

There is a lot of silence. "Where are you from originally?" he asks finally.

"From Yugoslavia," I reply.

"Good, I was afraid you were German."

"No, my mother read a book while she was pregnant. The heroine's name was Inge and here I am." It is so easy to talk to him. We have been talking for a half an hour. I know he is in the television business. I know that he has a house in Connecticut. Sounds good. Does he want to meet me?

"How about meeting next Tuesday at four for tea?" he says finally.

"I would love to. How will I know you?"

"Well, I am bald and what little hair I have is gray. What do you look like?"

"I am vivacious, slender and attractive," I say with a smile. "I will be wearing a mink coat. My hair is brown."

"I will find you," he says. "See you Tuesday!"

◊

I step out of the elevator in the lobby of my apartment building and there he is: bald, with gray hair, what there is of it, wearing a full-length sheepskin coat. The friendliest smile and kindest eyes. I come closer. "You look so familiar!" I hear myself saying.

It is a bitterly cold night in February 1986 in New York City. He holds open the door of his maroon Saab for me. I settle in. It seems so natural. Don takes his seat behind the wheel and looks at me. "I am sure we have run into each other somewhere. In this life or perhaps in a previous one." I look at him surprised. What bullshit. I don't really believe in a previous life and yet, he sounds so convincing.

Dinner in a small, very noisy French restaurant on East 34th Street is lovely. We talk incessantly but cannot hear each other too well. "This is no fun," Don remarks. "Let's have dessert somewhere else."

We walk a few blocks to a hotel on Park Avenue, where, according to Don, there is a quiet bar. As we enter, we pass the dining room. It seems to be closing. I notice a dessert tray with a bowl of fresh strawberries. "I love strawberries!" I exclaim. "That is what I would like."

The maitre d' tells us that the dining room is closed. "Sorry but there are no more strawberries available tonight." I know I look disappointed and I see Don pressing a $5.00 bill into the maitre d's hand. "We will be in the bar," he announces.

We sit down at a small, quiet table and as if by magic a large dish of strawberries appears. If Don meant to impress me, he succeeded. What a determined man.

"Who are you? Where do you come from?" Don wants to know all about me. I talk and talk. He inspires confidence. I seem to reveal more of myself than he does. Is he being cautious? Am I being too open?

By the end of the evening, Don convinces me that he saw me in Rome in 1973. "At the time I was shooting TV commercials in Rome and often went to the Café Greco with my girlfriend. It was definitely you I saw there one day."

It is true that in 1973 I lived in Rome with my husband, Frank. I went to the famous old café on Via Dei Condotti, near the Spanish Steps. It was *the* meeting place for an aperitivo or espresso with one's friends. It is possible that he saw me there. We also discover that at a certain time in 1963 we both lived on East 63rd Street, one block from each other. What a coincidence. We talk until one in the morning when the waiter politely tells us that the bar is closing.

Next morning, the ringing of the phone wakes me. It look at the clock: 8 A.M. "Well, how did it go?" my friend Maja asks.

"I think he is great. Nice, intelligent, easy to talk to. Cultured, good sense of humor, everything. I hope he calls me again. He is well worth knowing better."

A week has passed and Don has not called. I saw J. for dinner. What a difference. More than ever I know he is not for me.

"Hello." It is Don's voice. Finally! "Can I see you on Tuesday for dinner? Why don't you come to my apartment for drinks. About six?"

"To your apartment? I barely know you."

"Come on, don't be a child. Grow up." He sounds amused.

When I tell Renate and Maja, my dearest friends, that I am going to a man's apartment on our second date, they both flip. "I want to know the name, address and telephone number of the man." Renate's voice is very firm. "You don't know him at all, how can you be so trusting?" I feel like a child being scolded by her mother. I give her the information and of course go.

◊

The apartment building on East 9th Street is quite elegant, concierge and all. After being announced, I take the elevator to the 14th floor. Don is already waiting for me at the elevator door, dressed informally. We hug briefly and walk down a long corridor to his apartment. As soon as I enter I know he has taste. It is a small apartment, exquisitely furnished. A few paintings, prints by Ben Shahn, Dali. On one wall, photographs taken on his many trips, he tells me. Book shelves full of books, records, tapes and awards for best direction in commercials, one from Venice, another from Cannes. I am quite impressed. Don does not seem to give it importance, "I had more, used them for target practice."

We have drinks and pleasant conversation. It turns to psychology. "My mother is a psychiatrist," I tell Don, perhaps to impress him. "I myself am not much into it, perhaps as a reaction to hearing about it all the time."

"Have you read *Memories, Dreams, Reflections* by Carl Jung?" asks Don.

"I'm afraid not," I answer.

"I would like you to read it. Please take it home," he says.

"OK," I say, pleased that he apparently wants to see me again.

After a while he asks, "Are you hungry?"

"I sure am," I say. As we get up, I take the book.

"Why don't you leave it here? We will be back after dinner."

"We will?" I look at him, but he looks innocent.

We walk a few blocks to an Italian restaurant called 'Pirandello,' an 'in' place, Don tells me. As we sit down, the waiter greets Don in French. He must come here often. But French in an Italian restaurant? Oh, well! Food is good and so is the conversation. We seem to have much to talk about. I drink a lot of wine.

By the time we get back to the apartment I don't feel any pain. For some reason I say, "Could I have a cognac, please?" What is the matter with me?

"I hope you don't mind but I have to lie on the couch," says Don. "It's my back." Don comes over and lies down at the far end of the couch facing me.

"What is wrong with your back?" I ask, not sure I should believe him.

"I injured it four years ago. I was playing macho. I

carried a heavy television console and fell on my back," Don tells me. "I broke some of my vertebrae and lay flat on my back for a month. Some of the vertebrae fused together and as a consequence I am 3½ inches shorter than I used to be."

Well, no one could invent this story, I am thinking. And just as I start feeling comfortable again I feel Don's hand creeping slowly up my leg. I like it. What am I thinking? I hardly know the man, or do I? It seems I have known him for a long time. He looks at me in a strange way. "Let's go!" I hear myself saying.

How did I ever get into the bedroom, into bed? Well, here I am and it is wonderful. It feels great. "Are you all right?" Don holds me very tight.

"Perfect," I answer.

"Can you stay the night?" he asks.

"I am sorry, I cannot. I wear contact lenses and have no container to put them in, or glasses to wear."

"Next time?" Don's voice is questioning.

"Yes, of course."

Some time later Don hails me a cab, opens the door and kisses me goodbye. It is 3 A.M. I lean back and try to relax. Why did I do it? Second date.

What is he going to think? I try to get my thoughts straight. I know why I did it! I like him so much that I had to find out. If we don't click in bed, might as well end it before I fall in love. I found out. We are perfect. *Una questione di pelle,* the Italians say. A question of skin.

I see J., the lawyer, Saturday night for dinner. Don had told me that he was seeing a woman named Lois, someone he also met through the magazine, so I feel free to see J. I definitely want to be on an even footing with Don.

A few days later I do stay the night. This is our first waking up together. "We fit perfectly," Don remarks. Taking a shower together seems quite natural. As we leave the apartment for breakfast, Don says, "Seems as if we have always been together."

◊

I am living in a daze. Don is wonderful. Calls me every day. He is still seeing Lois sometimes. I wonder why? I have dinner with J. once a week. I really cannot stand his company. Don must be the right man for me. I have no doubts. Especially when A. calls me and asks me out for dinner, I reply, "How about lunch?" I think about my long-standing secret affair with A. I never thought I could ever be completely free. Too many memories. Good ones and bad ones. Well, now I hope I am free. Hallelujah.

As happy as I am, or is it because of it, guilt feelings start disturbing my peace of mind. Poor Frank. If he had not died I would never be so independent and happy in a new relationship. It doesn't seem fair. "Why don't you go see a therapist?" Don suggests.

I promptly agree. I need to talk to someone. Too many things have been going on since Frank became ill and died. At Don's recommendation I make an appoint with Lou Casata. I like him at once. He is tall, good looking and Italian. I always had a weakness for Italians. He is dressed in khaki shorts, open shirt and sandals. Strange attire for New York in April. I hope he is competent.

"Please sit down." He sits across from me. "Tell me about yourself." It seems very easy to talk.

"Well, I have been a widow for almost two years. I met Don and I am in love."

"Does he love you?"

"I believe so, except he keeps seeing another woman. When he is with me he is all mine. For some strange reason it does not seem to bother me too much. What I am really worried about," I continue, "are feelings of guilt. I am so happy. I feel so free. It doesn't seem right." I try to explain it all. Lou is very understanding. The session goes well and I make another appointment.

For Passover night I am invited to Long Island at Frank's family's house. I take the train from Penn Station together with a cousin of Frank's, Harry and his wife, Bette. He is a psychologist and graphologist, a serious one. I have two letters for him to analyze: J.'s, all typewritten except for his signature, and Don's.

As the Long Island train is rushing on towards Roslyn Estates, Harry looks at J.'s signature and dismisses it almost at once. "Stay away, he is childish, prone to temper tantrums, not too reliable." Then he reads Don's letter. His face brightens up. "He is a wonderful man, very artistic, warm, in need of affection, kind. Demands a lot of space. Don't push him. He is a bit afraid. All will be well. You are extremely compatible," he offers at the end. I am flabbergasted. I have not told him anything about Don and he described him perfectly.

◊

"Lou," I say at our next session. "I am ready to give Don an ultimatum. It is either me or Lois, not both anymore. To tell you the truth, if he does not pick me, he is a fool!"

Suddenly, Lou gets up from his chair and shakes my hand. "Congratulations Inge, you have done it. You really don't need me anymore!"

◊

It is a few weeks later, June 16, 1986. Don is driving me to the cemetery in New Jersey. It is two years to the day that Frank died. We walk up a small hill surrounded by trees. We pass my father's grave. I stop to put a small pebble on the headstone. A Jewish ritual. In the same row is Frank's grave. I stop to see if all is well kept, put a pebble on his headstone and meditate for a while. So many emotions whirl inside my chest. "FRANK T. September 3, 1917 – June 16, 1984." It is a grave for two. The headstone is meant for both of us. Do I really want to be buried next to him? He was my noncommunicative companion for 34 years. Some good. Some bad. No hard feelings. I am happy now!

I turn around to Don, but he is gone. I walk slowly down the hill towards the road. There he is, my darling, his eyes full of tears. "Why are you crying?" I say surprised. "You never met the man!"

"I am sorry," he whispers. "I am sorry that he had to die so I could have *you*."

◊ ◊ ◊

In this story Inge gives us a wonderful picture of two people, both youthful and optimistic, who meet late in life. In other stories, they discover striking similarities: Each is European, Don born in Germany but raised in France, Inge born in Yugoslavia; both spent the war years on the run from the Nazis, Don as a member of the French resistance, Inge with her family traveling through northern Italy one step ahead of capture.

Inge's stories move forward with no wasted words. There is a pleasing balance between narrative, dialogue, and inner thoughts and feelings.

SELECTION NINE

DRIVING MISS ANNE
by Anne Freedman

ONE HUNDRED PERCENT," SAYS THE DEPARTMENT OF Motor Vehicles checker as she hands me back my written test. That was the easy part. I am nervous as I stand in line for the eye test. I have macular degeneration and my vision is gradually deteriorating. I think I am still a safe driver, but they won't care what I think. In 1986, the examiner told me, "You sure have bad eyes!" But she gave me a four-year renewal.

When my turn comes I can make out the first five figures in the machine, but after that everything is a blur. "You have failed the test," the examiner says. "Get your doctor to fill out this form and bring it back here. Maybe you need new glasses."

I am disappointed, but not overly concerned. I feel sure things will work out. My ophthalmologist fills out the form and I learn that my vision is 20/70 in my good eye, 20/400 in the other. He says my condition is stable and he recommends a two-year renewal. I suppose I shouldn't have expected four years. Two is better than one—or none.

I return to the DMV with my form and stand in the vision test line again. I hear the man ahead of me complain to the examiner: "But my doctor said...." The examiner cuts him off. "We don't care what your doctor said. You have to pass our test."

I begin to worry. I repeat the eye test with the same result as before.

"Take this paper to Window 8 and make an appointment for a road test," says the examiner. I do this and go home to wait a week for my test. There's no reason to be upset, I tell myself. I've been driving for over 60 years. There's no way I couldn't pass a road test. Still, the unpleasant thoughts won't leave me. They occupy my mind at night. I can't fall asleep.

How could I manage without driving? My independence is threatened. Its all very well to say I could hire a driver or take a taxi or a bus. That involves other people and planning ahead. I'm not Miss Daisy, with a chauffeur on call at all times. The precious freedom of going out in the car when I feel like it and not when someone else feels like it is gone.

Since my husband's illness and death, I have thought a lot about growing old, about having to become dependent, about losing my freedom, my privacy. I have tried to get used to the idea of this kind of future, but it wasn't supposed to confront me yet. I'm not ready.

Finally the test day arrives. I sit in my car, number seven in the row of drivers waiting for the two examiners. This gives us plenty of time to hone our nerves. I have been careful to put new batteries in my hearing aids. Poor vision is bad enough. I don't want to complicate the situation.

A jaunty young woman slips in beside me. "I will not ask you to do anything illegal," she says as we drive off. I drive smoothly; I use my turn signals; I back up properly and I make a three point turn. I think I have done well as we return to the DMV office.

"You got 68," says the examiner. "70 is passing. You didn't look over your shoulder; you relied entirely on your mirror. That's dangerous. You will have to repeat the test."

I am crushed. I can't believe it. I always looked over my shoulder in my previous car, but in this one I can't see anything. The headrests are in the way. I suppose I shall have to pretend. If I told her the problem, she might want some structural changes in the car.

I go to my daughter's house and tell her about the road test. "Well," says Ceel, "you'll probably pass it the next time, but why don't we start looking anyway for a place near here for you? I'd like to have you closer and so would the children. I wish you could live in the house in back of us and just step through the fence when you wanted to go in the pool." I feel comforted. I don't want to move, but it feels good to be wanted.

A friend shows me how to lower the headrests and I see better, but not as well as I'd like. I practice looking over my shoulder at every opportunity. I begin to have nightmares. Should I sell my house and move closer to my daughter's? There is good bus service in Santa Monica. But I like my house and all the space I have. I like my garden. I really don't want to move. My thoughts are churning. I go to bed, but sleep doesn't come. I spend half the night reading or doing puzzles.

Friends try to reassure me. Surely I'll pass next time. But I don't want to be reassured. That's not where my concern is. I hope I pass the second test, but even if I do, it's only a reprieve. In a year or two I'll be facing the same problem. Sooner or later loss of independence will come. It's stalking me and I'm fighting it. I hate it. I hate to ask for help. But if this future is inevitable, shouldn't I learn to prepare for it instead of denying it? I think I've handled my hearing loss realistically. I don't try to hide it. So now I must be like Jacob, wrestling with my angel until I can be at peace with whatever my future will be. No one can do this for me.

I pass my second road test with the admonition not to spend so much time looking over my shoulder! So now I am free until 1992. But wait. It isn't over. They can't find the results of the vision test nor my doctor's report. I must take the eye test again. The results do not change. At least I'm consistent.

"Your vision is so poor I think we'll have to restrict your driving to sunlight hours," says the sympathetic examiner. "Is that all right with you?"

"Well, no," I reply. "I sing in a church choir one night a week . . . . "

"Well, all right," she says, "just be careful," and she renews my license for two years.

I go home and fall asleep in the middle of the afternoon. That night I sleep ten hours. The next night I sleep another ten hours. I guess I'm not the invincible, nerveless person people tell me I appear to be. But now I have two years to struggle with my angel, and I had better not procrastinate!

◊ ◊ ◊

Anne's story is filled with poignant humor as she addresses that which we all must face sooner or later: getting older and losing our independence. In facing it, she helps us see and prize it all the more. Her style is an understated mix of dialogue, narrative, and inner thoughts and feelings that bespeak her New England roots.

SELECTION TEN

YOU CAN'T ALWAYS
GO HOME AGAIN
By Selma Lewin

THIS IS LOS ANGELES ON A WARM SUMMER EVENING.
I have lived at this general location, in this once
highly desirable upper-middle-class Wilshire area, for
many years. Forty, as a matter of fact. I am astonished
to realize how much time has passed, how firmly circumstances have planted me here, and how things
have changed. I have been an owner, then a tenant and
now manager.

It is a congested, predominantly Latino neighborhood, and on this balmy evening people are in good
spirits, ebullient and jolly, because it's Friday night
and the first of the month; it's payday and Social Security and welfare checks and food stamps. Though most
people here work very hard at low-paying jobs, many
are illegal aliens and work on the "QT."

There is much laughing and calling out to one another. The man next door thrusts his head back and
guffaws in response to some funny remark hollered out

from a window. Everyone laughs. There is no way I can join in the fun. I am a foreigner in my own country.

Children are playing ball on the sidewalk, good old American ball, but they are playing in Spanish. The kids will not be called into bed until eleven, twelve o'clock at night. Whoever has remained indoors is blasting radio and TV in Spanish, at unendurable decibels.

In the building next door there are thirty-two apartments, singles, and if each single housed one occupant there would be thirty-two people. But although these apartments consist of one large room, kitchenette and bath, the usual occupants are two adults and two or three kids, even three kids and an infant on the way. So you have possibly 150 souls, a little community by itself in this one building next door.

They haven't much, but always plenty to throw away. On Wednesdays the boulevard is lined with old chairs, sofas with escaping stuffing, broken TVs, burned skillets, etc. The avenue of discarded mattresses.

Many have broken down (very broken down) cars and no garages. This causes conflict with my tenants who can't get out of our driveway due to illegal parking. They are always polite. "I'm sorry," they say after much blasting of horns from our tenants. It's a big, ongoing problem. The block is just too crowded, especially the big apartments like the building next door. How do they manage? How do they conduct their conjugal life? This always puzzles me. But that they do is patently apparent; so many smiling young mothers-to-be. Some so young they look about fifteen. Babies having babies.

The kids are cute, out playing like all kids, but they play in Spanish. I don't understand. Don't they go to school? One young mother who speaks some English told me she speaks only Spanish to her children because she does not want them to lose their culture.

What about my culture? Will I lose it? What will really resolve the bilingual question?

The children are sweet but uncharming when they answer nature's call right on the sidewalk. "Hey," I said to a seven-year-old, "Why don't you go upstairs? Or at least behind a bush?" "It's a free country," he told me. True. There was something uplifting about his having caught the American spirit. A free country. I tried to explain that freedom must be protected, at least to the extent of making wee-wee indoors, using the facilities provided for such an emergency. And not just the kids. I have seen grown men commit this transgression not too discreetly and, most puzzling of all, just after having come out of a building.

Part of the culture? Overcrowding, poverty, disenfranchised, ethnic? It is easy to see why countries have problems with ethnic diversity; ethnic diversity doesn't go down that well in our own country.

Odd, illegal businesses spring up overnight. A panel truck is parked illegally on the lawn festooned with clothing, blouses, shirts and skirts. Little girls' party dresses, pink and lacy. A hand-painted sign says, "Ropas Baratos," and, in concession to a non-Latino buyer, "Close Cheep."

Another business couple have stacked pillows on the grocery lot, against the wall under the graffiti. A tenant in one of the buildings has decided to market her homemade tamales. She sits on the stoop besides her large cauldron of tamales, wearing an apron with a big pocket for change, and hawks to the passersby, "Tamales! Tamales!"

A group of people are sitting on my lawn, as if it were a park, eating tamales. They do not live here. And where will they leave the wrappers? Am I a misanthrope to be disturbed by this? But where *shall* they sit? Many of the buildings where they live are flush with the street; there is no lawn. I try to be understanding.

A teenager toots his horn loud and long, summoning a friend. Horn blowing is a major problem here. Most do not have phones, and no place to park results in a lot of nerve-wracking horn blowing all hours of day and night. I ask this young fellow to tone it down. Most of the young people are polite and respectful but this one answers with a four-letter Anglo-Saxon expletive. "Oh," I say, "I see you are learning English."

A woman walks by, hands swinging at her sides, carrying a large bundle on top of her head. It does not impede her stride. Amazing. "Tamales! Tamales!" It goes on.

A bazaar, Mardi Gras atmosphere, exotic and lively. But I am lonely. With my limited Spanish and my own cultural background there is not much communication. It is as though I have been on a vacation to Mexico and now I want to go home. And once again I must remind myself—I am home. This is home?

◊ ◊ ◊

Selma gives us a vivid sense of her neighborhood as it is—with its pungent smells and earthy sights—and as it once was—uncluttered by the sounds, sights, and smells of another land. Her lively descriptions and dialogue coupled with her wry comments tell us what she feels she has lost and how she is learning to cope.

FIRST DAYS
by E. S.

I DIED ON JULY 9TH, 1984, IN LOS ANGELES, AFTER a brief illness. I do not remember much pain, although the violence of the infection that caused my death must have brought acute discomfort and consuming fever. I do remember, though, when I knew I would not live. My doctor had given me an injection and I felt suddenly pure and without substance. More than that, I saw my room, a nurse, my doctor, from an angle not at all relative to the position of my bed. They seemed farther away and lower, as if I myself were slightly levitated. Then I saw myself, one arm dangling over the edge of my bed and Janet, my wife, holding my hand. She was sitting on a chair, bent toward me.

It was confusing, for although I seemed above and out of myself, I could still feel the warmth of Janet's hand and see the look in her eye. I must have been like an image split in two when one's eyes, fixed on it, are out of focus... a candle flame that becomes two identical flames. Like a faint voice on a telephone, Janet's voice was saying, "You're doing fine, Ed. You're doing fine . . . ." She looked gray with fatigue, and her mouth, usually so pliant, seemed to have difficulty forming the words; but her eyes were the reflection of my own knowledge. They said, "He is dying."

I could not speak, but I matched the dishonesty of her words by smiling. It must have been a poor smile, because Janet's head sagged on my arm and the nurse turned her face away.

Then it happened. I remember one final spasm. And I remember thinking to myself, this must be the delivery of my soul; and I saw then a primitive Italian painting in reds and blues, where, from the prostrate body of a noble lord, escapes the white smoke of his spirit, freed. But there was this strange addition: I was for the time both the bearer and the born, the issuant and the issue. I was at the same moment creating and being created, and I could not tell which was the more difficult—the black fighting up into the light, or the more familiar expulsion of my burden.

But that is only part of the story. So much happened in what must have been so short a time that any ordered description is misleading. And yet the only way I can convey the simultaneous rush of sensations is to tell each of them one after the other, although they are no more separate than the separate colors that go to make up white. And I shall have to use the world's arbitrary measurements of time—days, weeks, months —to parcel out this chronicle of space.

First, with a fearful roar and clanging, as if a thousand metal hearts were beating against their walls, I was whirled into an emptiness as crowded with substance as are certain silences with sound. It was a wild and headlong flight, where I spun and reeled and palpitated like a leaf in a hurricane. In all this roaring and palpitating there was music . . . voices, phrases, instruments engaged in some gigantic prelude (to what symphony?). And there were words: fragments of poems; and through them all I, myself, screaming (to whom?) "Hold me!"—for the loneliness was terrible.

And Janet held me. Rather, she held a shell, for I had slipped out of it, as a hand from a glove. My body lay there, completely still. But it had no more to do with me than the starched white cap of the nurse who went to Janet and gently tried to pull back her shoulders. Janet raised her head slowly and looked with blind eyes toward the door. My doctor, standing there, moved toward her.

The headlong rush, the wheeling and roaring, stopped and a great silence came. I seemed to be quivering like a seismographic needle suspended in a stationary dance. This took place in an electric and impalpable void that had no boundaries. The nearest visual quality of this void is the queer light that one can see when the eyes are tightly shut against the sun. I was not alone. In this featureless state, there was a definite pattern of which I seemed to be only one point of many. This, presumably, was the final breakdown of matter.

A great peace settled over me. I had not realized until this moment how heavy was the burden of identity. This is the end, thank God, of Edward Scott; the end of this terrible and vigilant consciousness ... the end of doubt, of pain, of error; the end, even, of emotion; and the beginning of freedom.

As usual, I was a fool.

◊

I should not have been surprised, therefore, to find myself present at my funeral. The few times Janet and I talked of death, I'd raged against funerals. "For heaven's sake, don't give me one if I die. I think funerals are barbaric and miserable; it's destructive to true memory."

Janet laughed at me as if I were a willful child. "Okay, dear—we'll just dump you into the nearest ditch!"

I was dumped, instead, into a non-denominational church at Forest Lawn, in a very elaborate casket. The church was crowded, which surprised me. Janet, Jon, and Victoria were in the first pew, of course. Behind them were assorted cousins, aunts and uncles; Janet's brother and sister and their children; Emma, our cook of so many years. I recognized many friends, but there were many more I did not recognize. In the back pew of the chapel sat Laura. There were shadows under her eyes and she seemed very, very tired.

The altar was covered with flowers. At the right of it, the organist waited at the keyboard, his head turned to watch the cortege. At a signal from the head usher, the organ began to play the choral prelude, *Ich Ruf Zu Dir.* Jon must have arranged that, for we heard it together when he was thirteen, and at the end I had asked what he thought of it. After a pause he had said, "I guess that's religion." I told him it was mine; then added, half to myself, "I'd like to die listening to it."

The pallbearers were carrying my coffin slowly up the aisle. Laura did not look at the coffin. Neither did Jon. The boy was fixing his eyes, enlarged but dry, on an organ pipe. The only movement I could see was his collar working up and down on his thin neck. His hands were closed so tightly into fists, hanging at his sides, that the knuckles were white. His inaudible voice kept saying, over and over, "This isn't Dad, this isn't Dad."

Janet, correct and grave, followed the cortege with her eyes, and so did Victoria. Mourning became my wife; it refined her face and gave her bearing dignity. I think she was too tired to feel much, except a kind of incredulity. Over and over, she said, "My husband is dead. My husband is dead"—as if to convince herself of something she doubted. As for Victoria, my daughter, her stepdaughter, tears were streaming down her face. But they were not tears of uncontrollable grief. As clearly as if she were speaking above the crowd in her girl's voice, the words came out: "I have no father. He was famous and everybody is here and looking at me. I look like him. I am all in black and very pale and everybody is saying, 'Poor child, how like her father.'" All that Laura whispered was, "Stay with me."

I suppose, in spite of my aversion to funerals, mine could have been called a simple and unpretentious one. With few exceptions, these people had come to grieve for and honor me; with few exceptions, they loved me in their own separate ways. The dissonant notes (and I heard them as clearly as if the organist had struck them) came from two others besides Victoria, my daughter. There was Janet's sister, Julie, whose abiding reaction was, "Thank God Janet's free of that man." And there was Elly, my cousin, who considered my early death as a sort of fitting answer to what she had always believed was an amoral and indulgent life. When the three of them got together in the vestibule after the service was over, muttering to each other about the "tragic loss," it was a wonder that a gigantic projection of my smile did not alarm them into silence.

I must explain that this extraterrestrial eavesdropping of mine was accompanied by a complete absence of emotion. As far as I can see, this was a sort of compensation for total vision, which in life would have been unbearable. It was as though I were looking down at a borderless oriental rug of infinitely complex design. I could see each part in relation to every other part. I could see the deer stepping through the flowers and, at the same time, the man raising his bow to shoot at it. I could see the arrow speed and the deer stricken. I could see the river winding among the hills and the women drinking at its source. I could see two men fighting and one of them dead. The light was the same all over; nothing was in shadow.

There was, of course, no element of time. Or rather, past, present, and future co-existed exactly as they do in the world "today." In these early stages of seeing without feeling, I thought to myself, "This is Heaven." Later on I said, "This is Hell."

Will had died with my body. I was totally at the beck and call of those who remembered, needed, and wanted me. They re-created me in their own wills, they conjured up my presence, they plucked me out of my crowded electric void and gave me shape, if not substance. And, how long this slavery to the living (for that is what it was) would last, I could not tell. I was often in three or four places at once, especially in the weeks immediately following my death. The continuity of this record is, therefore, an arbitrary one.

I was a fool to think that any such drastic transition could be completed all at once, any more than an adolescent can become wholly mature overnight. Like every growth, it was a slow process. And it was to be a long time before I could really leave my life, before the severance from the world I knew was final.

◊ ◊ ◊

In this remarkable vision of his future, "E." shows us what it might be like to move from actuality into another plane of existence. He is able to look back at the living and wish they would simply let go of those who are moving on.

SELECTION TWELVE

MEMORIES
by Judith Klein

JUDY? THIS IS VICKI."

"Vicki, how are you? Is anything wrong? Is your mother okay?"

"Everything is fine. I just had to call you. Florrie gave me your stories to read and they are wonderful! I can't believe how much you remember. Reading them made Florrie and me start to reminisce." My cousin from New Jersey whom I haven't heard from in ages makes me smile. We exchange family conversation. It is so good to talk to her.

I had given my cousin Florrie a copy of "Backward Glances," our class journal, to take to my brother Billy in New Jersey. Florrie and Stanley had been out this way for a vacation and since she was so much a part of my early childhood, I let her read my stories.

"These are great," Florrie said. "I remember those times. Have you sent these to Billy yet?"

"No, as a matter of fact, I didn't think anyone would want to read them. I didn't think they were so great—just some of my memories put down on paper for my kids and my grandchildren."

"Are you kidding?" She is so enthusiastic and for Florrie, that's a lot. "Billy would love to read these."

"So maybe you'll take them to him for me?" I ask her, knowing there is a cousin's club in New Jersey and she will be seeing Billy before I could mail the book to him.

"Of course," she says. "He'll get a real kick out of reading these, I'm sure. And the other cousins, too."

The book has been in New Jersey for a few weeks now and Vicki is my first phone call.

"I took the book from Florrie and copied your stories before she gave it to Billy," Vicki says. "I didn't know you were such a wonderful writer."

I laugh. "To my mother, I'm a wonderful writer. To a writer, well, that's another story!" She laughs.

"Hang on, my mother wants to talk to you." Vicki's mom, Aunt Kate, is my mother's youngest sister and the only one alive on my maternal side.

"Judy, what a memory you have! We've been reading your stories and my girls have been asking me for more stories. This has been wonderful." Aunt Kate sounds so happy. She has been very sick lately.

"Do you remember those times?" I ask Aunt Kate.

"Of course! Everything is like I'm back there in time. I can see our bungalow in Coney Island, I can feel that wind in Bayonne. You are some storyteller! And you've made me remember other stories as well."

Well, now, maybe I *am* a writer! My ego is sky-high and to hear the pleasure in her voice and know that I provided it is the high point of my day.

It is early in 1988 and I have just received an invitation to Aunt Kate's 80th birthday party in April. I won't be able to go and ponder what to send her for this special day. I decide to go through my stories and take the most poignant and have them copied. I write a poem and enclose it with the stories and send them to her.

She responds: "Judy dear, that was the best present. All your cousins want copies of these stories.
They loved being reminded of those times gone by. We
reminisced and reminisced. It was wonderful." I call
Aunt Kate after the party. There are two generations of
cousins at her party and even the older cousins seemed
to like my stories. It still is mind-boggling that people
actually enjoy my writing. Maybe I should write a play!
After all, my family is a lot nuttier than Neil Simon's or
Woody Allen's family! See, they've created a monster.
Now they're making me believe I really am a writer!

In June of 1988, Morty and I are in New Jersey.
Billy, my brother, has a cousin's club gathering at his
house in our honor. He has invited all our family, the
younger cousins from the club and the older ones, too.
And of course, Aunt Kate.

"You must keep writing," my cousin Sanford in-
sists. "Can't you just see Linda Lavin as Aunt Molly? Try
to write a play. Our family is funny and you can do it!"

My cousin Jeannie makes me feel so good. "I'm so
happy to see you and I love your stories. You know
Mossie doesn't come out for everyone and he was so
happy that Morty was here." I smile. It's true; her husband goes only where he likes the people!!

"Why don't you just send your stories to us as you
write them and we'll pass them around like a memory
newsletter?" Vicki suggests. "You know, I've made a
family tree." I wonder if my stories helped her?!

Cousins and family that Morty and I haven't seen
or heard from in years have come here tonight. It is
such a warm, happy time.

My cousin Myra approaches me. "You know," she
says, "I, too, have read all the stories you sent and once
again, *I* am left out! No one ever saw me growing up
and no one ever remembers me being anywhere. I'm
not in any one of your stories. But, that's the story of
my life, always left out."

Oh God, so now I'm responsible for her psyche, too. Well, I guess when I'm ready to share my most powerful moment, the story of my bout with polio, then she will see how much she *was* remembered and how very much a part of my life she is. I still have many stories to write. Someday I will be ready to share them.

◊ ◊ ◊

Judy gives us a warm sense of how family story-telling and writing can enrich and renew bonds among friends and relatives. Judy originally came to class to write about her lifelong experience coping with polio. She has chronicled much of her past in stories, which she sends to various members of her family.

◊ ◊ ◊

Now you have arrived at the end of this small journey. You have absorbed the techniques of writing from within, of writing in an authentic voice. You have reflected on the experiences and stages of your life, worked on your stories, and read a number of other stories that may have served as models for your own writing and rewriting. In the course of working with this volume, you have explored your own creativity—your ability to express what you have seen and felt in life—and have experienced the pleasure of writing well.

Perhaps you have also come to view the difficulties you've encountered in your life in a new light, gaining a new understanding of their meaning and a new respect for the ways in which you handled yourself in the circumstances. In the course of writing your life's stories you may also have given a great deal of pleasure to and provoked considerable thought and feeling in your readers and listeners.

Keep writing, and encourage those you love to do the same.

◊ ◊ ◊

BIOGRAPHIES

ROSALIND BELCHER

Rosalind was born in the deep South at an unkind time in history. Finding it difficult to make ends meet, the family moved north. By eighteen, Roz was in New York, slowly spiraling downward. A lonely Jewish concentration camp refugee looking for a friend after the death of his wife helped her turn her life around. She entered Synanon in the 1960s. Eventually graduating from college with a degree in social work, Roz has worked in the field of vocational rehabilitation for many years. She presently has her own company in this field, and teaches parent education and life story writing for the Los Angeles Unified School District.

EDWARD BOYLE

Ed came to class for a very short period of time, leaving to be near his children in Colorado. Ed joined the Navy early in WWII, serving aboard a minesweeper for most of his years in the service.

CAROL CUNNINGHAM

Carol was a housewife in her forties at the time of the writing of this story. She died very suddenly of a heart attack. This story was left by her bedside, unfinished.

LOUIS DOSHAY

Lou was born in New York City of Russian immigrant parents. His family was poor and he worked after school and on weekends to help make ends meet during the Depression years. After WWII, he married, had children, got a college education, and worked in the aerospace industry until he retired. He came to life story writing to leave a record of his life to his grandchildren and to begin writing science fiction.

EDITH EHRENREICH

Edith was born in Vienna and experienced a serene childhood until Hitler came to power. After her escape, she emigrated to the United States where she has been a public school teacher for most of her life.

ANNE FREEDMAN

Anne Freedman was born "into a classically WASP family" in Washington D.C., where her father was on the faculty of American University. Married at a young age to a liberal minister, she spent her early married life in Maine. Divorced, with a young child, she got into social work and moved to Los Angeles. She uses her stories as an opportunity to review her life and to leave something of herself to succeeding generations.

STELLA GOREN

Stella was born in a Midwestern family. Her father was a milkman and used to take Stella around with him on his route when she was very small. She writes vividly of her youth, of her days as a Marine during WWII, of 'the man who got away,' and of her relationships past and present.

LAURA GREEN

Laura Green is a pseudonym for a retired professor who vividly recalls graduating from college during the Depression and finding it difficult to get work as she sought to unionize the factories in New York City. She married, had children, and divorced, then in her forties went back to school. Receiving her Ph.D., she went into teaching, where she was labeled "the lovable radical" by her students.

GRACE HOLCOMB AND TED BROWN

Ted grew up on a sheep farm in Colorado during the depression years. The nearby town of Collbran was as rough and colorful as any western town of the 1880s. Part Native American, Ted spent a lot of time outdoors while growing up. He joined the army in 1940, and saw service in the Philippines as a point man on patrol. His unit was the first to liberate Manila and he saw first-hand the infamous death camps in the Philippines. At war's end he was hospitalized for jungle rot. Released from the army, he kicked around for sometime, eventually heading west for the hardrock mining in Death Valley during the fifties.

Eventually he met and married Grace Holcomb. They had one child and were divorced. Ted and Grace have remained close friends over the years, and Grace came to class "so that we would be able to tell the grandchildren about Ted's life."

JADE (pseudonym)

Jade grew up on a Borneo rubber plantation in the years before WWII. She came to the United States in the 1960s, is married and a mother. She came to life story writing to "review her life and leave something for the grandchildren."

JUDITH KLEIN

Judy was born in Newark, New Jersey. She spent her early, happy years learning to play the piano and enjoying her wise and caring mother. During the polio epidemic of 1949, she contracted the disease and spent much of the next year in an iron lung. The next few years were made less difficult by a deeply understanding mother who was determined her daughter would lead a normal life. Her mother's support and Judy's own will enabled her to date, work, fall in love, marry, have children, return to work, and enjoy her grandchildren. She came to life story writing intent on telling her story of overcoming polio. She wound up writing many other stories rich with her own brand of humor and insight.

NAT LEVENTHAL

Nat was born in Russia around the turn of the century. He learned his trade as a tailor at the age of six and immigrated to the United States at the age of ten. He worked in the sweatshops of New York City throughout his teens, slowly becoming a master tailor. He had his own shop in New York, eventually selling out because of the graft, corruption, and the presence of the Mafia.

MAX LEVIN

Max was born in Germany of an entrepreneurial father and an adaptable mother. A failed business in Germany persuaded the family to move to Egypt, where business was better. Returning to Germany shortly before the rise of Hitler, Max's parents saw the need to get out and were successful, though just barely. Max came to the class feeling blocked and unable to write, though he had begun a novel of his life ten to fifteen years earlier. Re-creating the stories of his childhood has helped him, and he is now taking risks, as is evident from the story "Some Vacation."

SELMA LEWIN

Selma was born in New York City of Russian immigrant parents. She came to California shortly after

WWII and moved into a pleasantly Jewish neighborhood. Over the years she has seen her neighborhood change from Jewish to Korean to Central American.

BARBARA LEWIS

Barbara is Carol Cunningham's older sister. She is an artist in New Mexico.

LUCY MACDOUGALL

Lucy was born in Brooklyn, New York. She married a writer shortly before WWII and moved with him to Los Angeles when he was hired to write *Objective Burma,* starring Errol Flynn. Always interested in writing, she began working at *L.A. Magazine* after her divorce. Life story writing gives her the opportunity to force herself to remain creative. Once into the process, she began to see how it helped her review and understand her life's path.

EUGENE MALLORY

Gene was born in Iowa on a farm near a town hard-hit during the Depression. He has always loved writing, and traces his forebears back to Sir Thomas Mallory. Eventually, Gene moved from Iowa to Los Angeles where he worked for North American Rockwell.

VERA MELLUS

Vera was in her nineties at the time her story was written. She was born and raised in North Dakota during the wild years at the turn of the century. After the death of her father when she was very young, she recalls her mother running a tent hotel in Marmar. She crossed the country in a stagecoach and grew up in Glendale under the care of an aunt when her mother could not care for all the children. She appeared in the first western movie shot in Glendale in 1917, was educated in Los Angeles, and taught school in the mining towns of Arizona. She later returned to Los Angeles, married, and raised two daughters. Bright, elegant, and wise, Vera came to the class "to leave something to my grandchildren." Vera died in 1989.

ROSE ROTHENBERG

Rose was born in Kiev, Russia. Her parents immigrated to Philadelphia, where her father worked at the Baldwin Locomotive Works. The Depression came early to her family and her father was laid off and never did find another job. Rose was forced to give up her ambition of being a teacher, going to work as an accountant. After her children were grown, she returned to school; however, her husband's death forced her to return to work once more. Rose came to class to write stories for her grandchildren.

ROSE SAPOSNEK

Rose was born in the Ukraine and lived on her grandfather's farm until he was shot during the turmoil of the Russian Revolution. She and her mother escaped through the Crimea, eventually landing in Cuba, where she grew up, married, raised children, and cared for her mother.

BESS SHAPIRO

Bess was born in New York of a Russian immigrant mother who had at one time acted in the Moscow Art Theater of Chekhov and Stanislavski. In the United States, her mother acted in the Yiddish theater, where she met and married a young actor/director. The family moved to Salt Lake City, where Bess was raised to be a pianist. Bess is the wife of Isidore Ziferstein and came to class to write stories for her grandchildren, primarily stories of her wise and beloved grandmother, who appears in "Advice to a Foolish Virgin."

CATHY SMITH

Cathy Smith is a pseudonym for a recently divorced woman in her forties who is currently finishing her B.A. degree. She met her husband at the university where she was an English major, and left college in 1966 to get married. She is an only child, as are both her parents, and has no children herself.

Born in Pennsylvania, she and her mother moved to Los Angeles after her mother's divorce from the step-father in this story. Cathy did not even remember the incident she wrote about until she was 22 and has never told her mother about it. She does not like the taste of fish and refuses to eat it.

JOHN STRONG

John is a big strapping man, 6′3″ and 240 pounds, from a patriotic family of Pennsylvania coal miners. Many of his ancestors fought for the Union during the Civil War, and John was brought up on stories of war and heroism. He writes vividly of this boyhood years growing up in Pennsylvania, of his young manhood as a coal miner during the Depression, of his disappointment at not gaining an appointment to West Point, and of his days as a soldier during WWII.

LILY TOKUDA

Lily was born in the United States but accompanied her terminally ill father to Japan where he chose to die among his family. She was educated at Catholic schools in Japan through high school. She returned to the United States just before Pearl Harbor. Reunited with her family, she was interned at Hart Mountain, Wyoming, where she met a young enlisted man visiting his relatives. They fell in love and within six months were married. She spent most of the war years on an army base. Her husband and his unit fought with bravery in

Italy, with over half of the unit dying during the campaign. After the war, Tadd found it difficult to find work, and began working as a gardener. Lily and Tadd have three sons. Her stories are written so the grandchildren will know about their grandparents.

INGE TREVOR

Inge was born in Yugoslavia. She spent the war years traveling from one Northern Italian town to the next, always staying one step ahead of the Nazis. Immigrating to the United States, she married a European corporate executive. For many years they lived in Rome. After thirty years of marriage, her husband died and Inge had to learn about aloneness and reentry into the world.

GINA WILCOX

Gina was born in Ohio of Serbo-Croatian parents. Her expansive, life-loving father died when she was young, leaving her overworked, poorly educated mother to care for a large family. Gina grew up in Long Beach during WWII, eventually working for a film studio. She married and raised three girls. An artist, Gina has had a number of exhibitions. She gives considerable attention and concern to the well-being of older adults. She came to the life story writing class to "keep her mind sharp."

HELEN WINER

Helen grew up in Minnesota where she met her husband when she was nineteen and he, an already prominent dermatologist, was twenty-nine. They moved to Los Angeles and she raised her family while her husband achieved international fame. She came to class to begin memoirs for her grandchildren, memories of her beloved husband, hospitalized with Alzheimer's disease.

DAVID YAVITTS

David, who is in his eighties now, grew up along the Mississippi River. His fondest childhood memories are of the rough and bawdy riverfront life of the early 1900s. David was for a time a professional gambler aboard the riverboats that plied the river.

ISIDORE ZIFERSTEIN

Isidore was born in the Ukranian village of Kitigorod. His father left for America when Isidore was very small. His mother continued to run the family general store, where Izzy sat on the counter listening to all the stories and observing all the people of his shtetl (village). After the Russian Revolution, the cossacks, units of the czar's army, roamed the Ukraine terrorizing the peasant Jews. Simon Petlyura's Haidamaki (troops) came to Kitigorod one day in 1918 and murdered most of its inhabitants. Isidore has written vividly of his memories of what happened all around him. Later Isidore and his mother came to America, where they rejoined his father, and he grew up in New York City. He attended Columbia University and received an M.D. in psychiatry, a profession he has practiced since the mid-1930s. Isidore came to the class to uncover and write about memories he had long suppressed, but which he felt his children and others ought to know.

Appendix I

Putting It All Together, Making A Book

HAVING FINISHED THE STORY OF YOUR LIFE, AN undertaking of many months, perhaps even years, you will want to put it together or "package" it in a way that will give you a sense of accomplishment and have a pleasing effect on those who read it. You've tackled the project as seriously as any artist would, and your work deserves to be mounted properly. Here are some hints about "wrapping it all up": illustrating your work, presenting each page in the most readable way, using calligraphy and ornamentation to enhance the work, reproducing and binding copies handsomely, and selecting an appropriate cover for the finished book.

Just as we anticipate with pleasure what will be found inside a nicely wrapped Christmas gift or birthday present, so the little extras which we add to our finished volume will give our readers a sense of anticipation and delight when they pick up our work.

PAGE DESIGN AND LAYOUT

Your narratives are worth preserving and should be as readable as possible. Unless you have a very readable and artistic handwriting, they should be typed or printed using a word processor or a personal computer with a good printer. The printer should have "letter quality" type. Be careful of dot matrix printers which look "computer-ish" and may not reproduce adequately; test them first to see that they have a letter-quality mode. And look into using laser printer facilities that are now available in many copy-and-quickprint shops.

If your work is typed, earlier drafts should be double-spaced, but the final version can be done with one and a half spaces. A one-inch margin should be allowed on three sides of the page, with an inch and a half for the left-hand, or inside, margin, where you will bind the book. Help the reader by treating special elements of the text, like poetry or quotations, in a special or distinctive way. One common technique is to indent these sections or elements about a half inch from the left margin. Always remember to indent the beginnings of new paragraphs, though it is not necessary to leave a whole extra line between paragraphs.

If you should decide to get your book laser-printed, find someone with an understanding of book design and typography to help you design the basic page layout. And if you have the book professionally typeset, always use a *book* typesetter, not someone whose main typesetting experience is with advertising or newsletters and flyers.

ILLUSTRATIONS

"A picture is worth a thousand words" is the old cliché, and it truly will enhance your work to include photographs, drawings, even carefully chosen memorabilia pasted up in the pages of your book. If you plan to have a number of copies of your life story made, you may make photocopies of the photographs and place them in the text. For better quality at a slightly higher cost, you could get duplicate photographs, or ask your local small printer to get you "photostats." Be sure to leave room in the text for the photos as you are typing it or printing it out, or ask a local graphic artist or graphic arts student to help you to "cut and paste" the final text.

A handmade drawing is another and very delightful type of illustration. One very creative idea was suggested in a class by a student writing the life of her mother. As she finished each story, she had her young daughter illustrate it with drawings. The resulting collection of stories with illustrations was given as a present to the student's mother on her birthday, and a second installment at Christmas time. It was a deeply heartfelt experience shared by three generations of a family.

TITLES AND HEADINGS

The first page of each story should be treated a bit differently. Book designers frequently use ornamental capitals or special sizes and typefaces for chapter headings and openings. As a basic page layout, you might start the title of the story one or two inches from the top of the page, and start your first line of text about two to three inches below the title. This is a generally used, fairly standard approach. You should feel free to make as many creative variations on it as you wish. For examples of some of the design elements we have talked about, look again at the treatment of titles, chapter openings, and page layouts in this and other books.

Another way of giving your narrative a nice look is to use calligraphy in appropriate places. Calligraphy, which is elegant, stylized handwriting done by specialists, can be used to nice effect as chapter or story headings, as in the following:

"Right You Are If You Think You Are"

Calligraphy or special designs can also be used as ornamentation, to give style to the first letter of a chapter or text:

HISTORIANS of art like to present the turn of the century as an Epoch and begin a new chapter even when describing Northern painting.

The reader may think calligraphy and ornamentation are too fancy for his or her narrative, but in fact they add a personal, handcrafted feel to a volume of stories and experiences that is itself very personal and handcrafted. So calligraphy is entirely appropriate in such a work.

A good way to find calligraphers and obtain advice about graphic design is to consult the list of course offerings at your local adult school, community college, or art school, or consult the art department of any high school or college in your area.

REPRODUCTION, COVERS, AND BINDINGS

At the present time, photocopying techniques allow one to reproduce one's work fairly inexpensively. Likewise, inexpensive, attractive covers and bindings may be obtained at most printing shops for a few dollars and will add a very nice appearance to your work. The commonly available binding options are *velo binding*, where the pages of the book have holes punched in them and a black plastic strip is attached on both sides that holds the book and covers together, and *comb* or *spiral binding*, where the pages and cover are held together by a broad comb, making it look rather like a spiral notebook. The velo binding is generally neater and has more strength; the comb binding is better for thick books and those that need to open up flat. To see examples of these bindings, go to your local copy shop, and select what looks and feels best to you.

More expensive binding options include *perfect binding*, where the pages are glued together inside a cover, and *case* or *cloth binding*, which is done using a hardcover case. These are generally too expensive for one, two, or even fifty copies of a book, but if you are interested, look in your local yellow pages under "bookbinders" or ask at your library for the name of a library binder.

APPENDIX II

TEACHING LIFE STORY WRITING IN THE CLASSROOM

IMPROVING LANGUAGE ARTS CURRICULA ACROSS THE NATION

UP TO THIS POINT, THE READER UNDOUBTEDLY HAS gotten the impression that writing from within is mostly the province of older adults looking back over their lives. True, this is the arena in which most of the techniques were developed. At the same time, I have developed and conducted college life story writing workshops which enable students to bridge the gap between high school and college, or in the case of returning students, to bridge the worlds of work and college. Writing from within techniques have worked as a powerful and effective first step to college level academic writing.

◊ It helps students with their fears of writing, how to recognize and cope with the critic when it appears.

◊ It helps students develop flexibility in writing style. Using the present tense, short sentences, and the like may or may not be appropriate, but it does build writing muscle.

◊ An awareness of form—strong opening, getting the readers to ask the right questions, finding and sticking to the spine, expanding the climax, achieving a balance of narrative and dialogue—applies to academic writing as well.

◊ Learning to write dialogue helps students understand the importance and use of firsthand experience in the same way that quoted material in academic writing gives authenticity, immediacy, and variety to lengthy narratives. Dialogue and quotes also give the reader an opportunity to see the material independently of the writer's thoughts about the material.

◊ The exercises of writing from different points of view, that is, the child's or two points of view of one experience, enable the writer to get out of himself or herself and get behind other points of view, one of the goals of academic writing.

◊ ◊ ◊

I have also worked with a growing number of teachers in grades five through twelve. Many states mandate the development of skills in narrative writing, and life story writing has much to offer these programs. The process of writing from within is, for example, entirely consistent with the recently instituted English Language Arts Framework developed in California.

Unfortunately, getting these techniques into the school system is not easy. Autobiographical writing is, for the most part, looked upon as a poor sister to critical writing, and even creative writing. It is thought of as "What-did-you-do-last-summer?" writing.

As I see it, there is a virtual black hole in the Language Arts curricula in most American public schools.

Vast numbers of students, faced with critical thinking and writing tasks, sink into a numbing darkness of confusion, incapacity, and panic. We educators wring our hands in despair. Why is it so? we ask. Is there anything we can do that we have not already done? One little-noticed reason for this dismal state of affairs is that students have skipped over a vital link in the learning-to-write process. They are asked to go at left-brain tasks too early, and too little attention is given to their need for writing which is relevant to their life's circumstance.

Life story writing as outlined in this book is a program that teaches tense flexibility, oral storytelling, dialogue development, and the like. By applying fiction writing and theatrical techniques to the memories of one's life, seen from the point of view of the age at which the event took place, dignity is given to the innocence of the child's point of view, while subtly building sophisticated skills. In this way, life story writing becomes a necessary precursor to critical thinking and writing tasks.

A PRACTICAL CURRICULUM

Teachers wanting to use some of what we have discussed in this book in the classroom can try the following:

1. Arrange the desks in a semi-circle (or two if necessary).

2. Ask students if they ever hear stories about their parents' and grandparents' lives *or* ask them what some of their favorite stories are. Discuss storytelling a bit.

3. Ask them how far back they can recall something in their own lives.

4. Have them tell their earliest recollections aloud. (Not their earliest vivid memory, but the very earliest thing they can remember.)

5. Have them retell the memory in the present tense (very important!!).

6. Encourage other class members to describe the difference between the two (usually the second will yield much more detail).

7. Have students write the memory down on paper (urge them not to stop until they have finished the draft).

8. Have students read the written memory aloud to the class.

9. Prompt listeners to describe the differences (only the positive ones) between the oral version and the written version (usually the latter has more detail).

10. Conclude the exercise with positive comments about how interesting even a small memory such as their earliest memory is.

Earliest Vivid Memory #1

11. Begin the next exercise on another day by repeating steps 1–10, asking students to recall their most vivid early memory from age 1–12 (they need not tell anything painful or embarrassing).

12. Have students rewrite the memory adding dialogue and feelings, as discussed in Chapters One, Two, and Three.

13. Distinguish between rewriting and editing, and have students edit final drafts of their stories, paying attention to grammar, spelling, etc.

14. Repeat the process until, after two or three memories, students are comfortable writing in the present tense without telling the story aloud.

15. Repeat the process. With each new vivid memory, an item from the checklist may be added to the process if students demonstrate sufficient skills in handling previous steps.

◊ ◊ ◊

The steps outlined here can be applied to every grade and every level from the fifth grade to the twelfth. Additional assignments may be found at the ends of the first several chapters of this book. Much exciting work could be accomplished by teachers simply using these steps in class.

For more accomplished students, the other techniques discussed in the book can be added. Establish a supportive non-critical atmosphere for the students and encourage them to learn the feedback techniques found in Chapter Seven. Distinguish between rewriting and editing. Grade the students' efforts only through continual praise. If grades must be assigned, reserve grades for the *editing* portion of the final draft, or average an A for the composing, reviewing, and rewriting phases into a grade for editing.

At all costs, students need to feel that our school systems value and appreciate their memories of their life's experiences and their expression and interpretation of these memories.

Here is a possible sequence of assignments which has proven to be very successful with college and older students.

1. Your earliest memory.

2. Your earliest powerful memory from birth to 10 or 12.

3. One to six more early powerful memories from birth to 10 or 12.

4. An interesting person memory.

5. A place memory.

6. A family history memory.

7. A powerful memory from each decade of your life.

8. A memory of an experience you share with another person—their experience and yours on paper.

9. Filling in the gaps: vivid memories from each of the decades of your life, beginning with half a dozen or so from your childhood

10. A letter of forgiveness to Mom or Dad.

To obtain more information and materials on teaching life story writing in schools and adult education classes, please use the order form at the back of this book, or write to the author, care of

Hunter House Inc., Publishers
PO Box 847
Claremont, CA 91711

A number of study curricula and workbooks are in preparation for teaching life story writing, and will begin to be available in 1991.

SELECTED READINGS

I. WRITING MODELS

Aiken, Conrad. *The Collected Short Stories* (New York, Schocken Books, 1982).
"Silent Snow, Secret Snow" allows us to glimpse a young boy's fascinating and very private world from his point of view.

Bierce, Ambrose. *The Stories and Fables of Ambrose Bierce* (Owings Mills MD, Stemmer House Publishers, 1977).
His stories "Occurrence at Owl Creek Bridge," "The Boarded Window," and "One of the Missing," provide us with superbly shocking, unpredictable, mind-teasing endings.

Campbell, Joseph. *Hero with a Thousand Faces* (Princeton NJ, Princeton University Press, 1973). *The Masks of God,* 4 volumes (New York, Penguin, 1970, 1976).
The path of the "hero" in all of us is traced through quests and temptations, weaving its way through virtually all of the world's mythologies and religions.

Doctorow, E. L. *World's Fair* (New York, Fawcett Crest, 1986).
Doctorow's novel, which displays a number of tech-

niques of life writing, chronicles the events and experiences of his fictional hero's life.

Dostoevski, Feodor. *Crime and Punishment* (New York, Bantam Books, 1984).
The author interweaves first person narrative, dialogue, and inner monologue in this classic story of risk-taking, crime, and conscience.

Dreiser, Theodore. *The Best Short Stories of Theodore Dreiser* (Chicago, Ivan R. Dee, Inc., 1989).
The narrator's voice in a Dreiser story is often clumsy and intrusive, a legacy of the nineteenth century, yet the stories are well worked out, often gripping and ironic.

Hemingway, Ernest. *Collected Short Stories* (Charles Scribners Sons, 1938).
Hemingway's narrator remains as discreet and inconspicuous as Dreiser's is heavy-handed. The author makes his points dramatically through dialogue and occasional inner monologue.

Ibsen, Henrik. *Complete Major Prose* (New York, New American Library, 1978).
The plot structure and the problems Ibsen sets for his characters and the qualities he gives them make his plays forever interesting.

Lang, Fritz. *M__* Classic Film Scripts, a series (London, Lorrimer Publishing, 1973).
In M, *we experience the forcefulness of the pursuers, including the protagonist's own conscience, from the point of view of the criminal pursued.*

Miller, Arthur. *Death of a Salesman* (New York, Penguin, 1977).
The struggle of a character to achieve a goal and the way he pursues it when he can't have what he really wants give Miller's play dignity and meaning.

O'Connor, Flannery. *The Complete Stories* (New York, Farrar, Straus and Giroux, 1971).
Ms. O'Connor offers some of the most bizarre and interesting characters in modern short stories.

Orwell, George. *Collected Essays,* 4 volumes, (San Diego CA, Harcourt Brace Jovanovich, 1968).
"Shooting an Elephant" is classic autobiographical writing—crisp narrative storytelling, a clear view of the objective world facing the writer, physical action, and reflection on the meaning of the actions one takes.

Pirandello, Luigi. *Plays* (Harmondsworth, Middlesex, England, Penguin Books, 1962).
Pirandello's plays bring us into a series of delightfully separate worlds in which each character is convinced his view of the "real world" is correct and each character manages to convince us he is right.

II. WRITING PROCESS

Capacchione, Lucia. *The Creative Journal* (Athens OH, Ohio University Press, 1979).

Clurman, Harold. *On Directing* (New York, Macmillan, 1983).

Goldberg, Natalie. *Writing Down the Bones* (Boston, Shambhala Publications, 1986).

Rico, Gabriele. *Writing the Natural Way* (Los Angeles, J. P. Tarcher, 1983).

Stanislavski, Constantin. *An Actor Prepares* (New York, Routledge/Theatre Arts, 1989).

Ueland, Brenda. *If You Want to Write* (Saint Paul MN, Graywolf Press, 1987).

III. AUTOBIOGRAPHICAL WRITING

Augustine. *The Confessions of St. Augustine* (New York, Mentor Books, 1963).

Dillard, Annie. *An American Childhood* (New York, Harper and Row, 1987).

Scott-Maxwell, Florida. *The Measure of My Days* (New York, Penguin Books, 1979).

Simon, Kate. *Bronx Primitive* (New York, Harper and Row, 1983).

Simon, Kate. *A Wider World: Portraits in an Adolescence* (New York, Harper and Row, 1986).

Wiesel, Elie. *Night* (New York, Bantam Books, 1982).

Wilde, Oscar. "Confessions," *Complete Writings of Oscar Wilde* 10 volumes (New York, Nottingham Society, 1907).

IV. GUIDES TO AUTOBIOGRAPHICAL WRITING

Kanin, Ruth. *Write the Story of Your Life* (New York, Hawthorn/Dutton, 1981).

Keen, Sam, and Fox, Anne Valley. *Telling Your Story: A Guide to Who You Are and Who You Can Be* (New York, Signet Books, 1973).

Hateley, B.J. *Telling Your Story, Exploring Your Faith* (St. Louis, CBP Press, 1985).

Moffat, Mary Jane. *The Times of Our Lives* (Santa Barbara CA, John Daniel and Co., 1989).

V. *LIFE STAGES*

Birren, James E., and Schaie, K. W. *Handbook of the Psychology of Aging* (San Diego CA, Academic Press, 1990).

Erikson, Erik. *The Life Cycle Completed* (New York, Norton, 1982).

Frankl, Viktor. *Man's Search for Meaning* (New York, Pocket Books, 1963).

Gribben, K., Schaie, K. W., and Parham, I. A. "Complexity of Lifestyle and Maintenance of Intellectual Abilities," *Journal of Social Issues* 365:47-61, 1980.

Maslow, Abraham. *Toward a Psychology of Being* (New York, Van Nostrand, 1962).

Olney, J. *Metaphors of Self: The Meaning of Autobiography* (Princeton NJ, Princeton University Press, 1972).

Schaie, K. W., and Willis, S. L. "Lifespan Development," *Encyclopedia of Educational Research* (New York, Macmillan, 1982).

Sheehy, Gail. *Passages: Predictable Crises of Adult Life* (New York, Bantam Books, 1977).

VI. *COLLECTIONS*

Walker, Scott, ed. *The Graywolf Annual Three: Essays, Memoirs and Reflections* (Saint Paul, MN Graywolf Press, 1986).

Zinsser, William, ed. *Inventing the Truth: The Art and Craft of Memoir* (Boston, Houghton Mifflin, 1987).

ORDER FORM

10% DISCOUNT on orders of $20 or more —
20% DISCOUNT on orders of $50 or more —
30% DISCOUNT on orders of $250 or more —
On cost of books for fully prepaid orders

NAME			
ADDRESS			
CITY		STATE	
ZIP		COUNTRY	

TITLE	QTY	PRICE	TOTAL
Everyday Racism *(paperback)*		@ $12.95	
Everyday Racism *(hard cover)*		@ $19.95	
Healthy Aging *(paperback)*		@ $11.95	
Healthy Aging *(hard cover)*		@ $17.95	
Lupus: My Search for a Diagnosis		@ $6.95	
Menopause Without Medicine		@ $11.95	
Raising Each Other		@ $7.95	
A Picasso On the Beach		@ $14.95	
Strømme		@ $14.95	
Send information about other Life Story Writing Materials			❑
Send information about book production services			❑

Shipping costs:
First book: $2.00
($3.00 for Canada)
Each additional book:
$.50 ($1.00 for
Canada)
For UPS rates and
bulk orders call us at
(714) 624-2277

	TOTAL	
Less discount @____%		( )
TOTAL COST OF BOOKS		
Calif. residents add sales tax		
Shipping & handling		
TOTAL ENCLOSED *Please pay in U.S. funds only*		

❑ Check   ❑ Money Order   ❑ Visa   ❑ M/C

Card # _____ Exp date _____

Signature _____

Phone number _____

Complete and mail to:
Hunter House Inc., Publishers
PO Box 847, Claremont, CA 91711
❑ Check here to receive our book catalog